The Novels of Kamala Markandaya and Ruth Jhabvala

The Novels of Kamala Markandaya and Ruth Jhabvala

A Study in East-West Encounter

REKHA JHA

PRESTIGE

PRESTIGE

Published by
Prestige Books
3/28, East Patel Nagar, New Delhi 110 008
in association with
Indian Society for Commonwealth Studies
New Delhi

ISBN 81-85218-15-3

Jacket design by
3-A Corporation,
New Delhi 110 002

Phototypesetting by
data culture
New Delhi 110 065
Ph. 6431070

Printed at
Mehra Offset Press
New Delhi 110 002

Contents

Introduction

The encounter of the West and the East is a prominent theme in Indian writing in English. It has wide ramifications that need a detailed and incisive scrutiny. The conventional polarity or antagonism between what is known as the East and what is looked upon as the West is indeed fast disintegrating in this increasingly scientific and de-spiritualized world. Nevertheless historically, philosophically, sociologically and even temperamentally, the East signifies a sort of orientation that cares eventually more for the inner and the unseen, the categorical and the absolute. These values are associated with, or may be interpreted as, passivity, stagnation, rootedness and a kind of conservatism that seems antithetical to progress and material attainments. The West likewise signifies a sceptical, hardheaded, if not cynical, attitude towards the problems of the world. The area of divergence between the East and the West therefore is readily identifiable and certain factors in operation in our age continue to accentuate these points of difference between the East and the West.

The East and the West were first brought together in trade. But it was really the imposition of the English language and education that caused this cultural dislocation.[1] The Indian mind was thereon exposed to western culture but being too self-conscious it could not submit to western impact completely. Numerous educational institutions for higher training opened the gates of western knowledge to many Indians. The intellectuals who received their education through the medium of English were naturally exposed to the discipline and ethos of English. They imbibed western values without really dissociating themselves from indigenous cultural traits. The contact therefore proved more nourishing than intoxicating.

It would be appropriate here to define this nebulous term, values, that seems to divide the people of the East and the West *en bloc*. Clyde Kluckohn, an American sociologist, says that the views of a given group regarding the structure of the universe, the relation of man to the universe and the relations of man to man represent the group's own definition of the ultimate meaning of human life.[2] The issue has even more succintly been summed up by Cora Du Bois in three questions.[3] She says that the total range of possible answers and the consistency among the answers to the questions of man's relation to nature, his conception of time and his relation to other men, constitutes the basic premises of varying value systems. These answers define the "way of life" of different groups of people.

In the East, man accepts the forces of nature as invincible. He looks back to the past as a lost golden age and Hinduism conceives of nature as the tragedy of life and evil as ultimately illusory. A strong enough feeling is therefore generated to accept and spiritually overcome the trials of existence on grounds of religion, hence the passivity, stagnation and acceptance. The West, on the other hand, believes that man can strive to master nature through the application of science in the form of technology. He can therefore look forward to an even more perfectible world that is in progress. Man in the West is an isolated individual charged with cherishing and developing his unique potentialities. But in the East man is a member of a strict hierarchical order where each must perform the duties allotted to him.

Indians educated in the western way (the numbers of which have greatly swelled) have grown up enlightened on western pragmatism and rationalism. But the roots of their native culture are nevertheless strongly entrenched in them. The fabric of contemporary Indian society is being constantly woven with the strands of indigenous traditions and imported western conceptions. Every educated Indian has become a product of the conflicts and reconciliations of this dual culture. The Indian writer in English, by his very choice of medium, indicates his awareness of and exposure to a culture other than his traditional Indian. His intimate experience of the alien culture makes him more conscious of his own Indianness. Aware of the differences in the two values and using for his communication the language of his adopted culture, he is seized with the need to interpret his native values to an audience ignorant of them. He is naturally engaged in the evaluation of his own attitude towards these two aspects of his being, so that it becomes necessary for him to dwell on this dialectical and contrastive theme. We may therefore say that the Indo-English literary situation is rooted in this cultural dualism.

Allen J. Greenberger points out that the English writers like Rudyard Kipling, who based their stories on India, also believed that there was a basic difference between the East and the West.[4] While the West believed in an active positive world, the East had a passive negative world. The English in India made no effort at understanding the Indian and vice-versa, so that there were negligible social relations between the two in that period of 1880-1910. The British, confident about the value of their own culture, believed that to succeed in their endeavour in India it was best to retain their own individual identity and so they rejected everything Indian. It was not desirable to forget that one was an Englishman first and foremost; so, while India was enjoyable as an experience one took care not to get involved with it. John Masters even confesses that they were "like people living in a room upstairs who knew nothing of what was going on in the house below." He felt that the only way "to feel India," stipulated that you must become Indian; gain one set of qualities and lose the other.[5] The English found this difficult to do. But the need then, as now, was the need for a "mutual assimilation of East and West without injury to either,"[6] as Mrs. Steel suggests. This indeed has been the greatest social problem the world has ever seen or is likely to see. It was in Markandaya's words, "too strident, too dissonant, too austere, too raw."[7] To become acceptable it had to be "muted, toned down, tarted up—its music larded with familiar rhythms, its literature wrenched into shapes recognized by Western tradition, its dances made palatable by an infusion of known idioms, its people taught to genuflect before understatement." The meeting was possible on a personal level only as long as the demand did not become inordinate and there was accommodation and co-existence.

Indo-English writers, having learned the art of the novel from their acquaintance with it in English literature, became chiefly concerned with how the East and the West came together to resolve consequent complications. Beginning with Sarath Kumar Ghose's *The Prince of Destiny* in 1909, Indian novelists of English fiction attempted to study this encounter at various depths. In Raja Rao, the East-West theme assumes a depth and validity in the quintessence of the *advaita* philosophy of Brahmanical India, to the exclusion of India at all other levels. The West is seen as insisting on the particular, the concrete, the personal and the immediate in its recognition of the object as something outside oneself. Mulk Raj Anand had made a quest of sociological problems. He examines the western ideas encroaching on Eastern traditions and declaims the latter. In his novels, India's medieval and aristocratic society is sought to be changed by the agencies of modernity like science, industrialization and liberal democracy in order to create a dynamic new society. He is, because of his western education, convinced of man's power to master nature through a rational technology; so while the old in his novels sit mourning their fate, the young look forward to a more perfectible world in the future. The East-West problem is viewed not so much on British-Indian aspects of the dilemma as the Indian-Indian conflicts. But the personal social problem is seen as a traditional East-West conflict. His uniqueness lies in his intertwining of the political and religio-philosophical aspects of the East-West dichotomy without neglecting the other facets.

R.K. Narayan is more concerned with translating the East-West dichotomy into Indian terms consonant with tradition versus change. In Bhabani Bhattacharya again, the East-West is viewed against "the frail old-world wheel of wood set against the giant machines of the modern age."[8] His novels aim at fulfilling the hopes and quests of Gandhi and Rabindra Nath Tagore in the "integration of the simple and the sophisticated; the ancient and the modern; city and village; East and West."[9]

Literature has given form and utterance to a people's hopes, despairs, enthusiasm and apathy. It mirrors their joys and pains. The Indian began at first with historical romances when the renaissance set in. A couple of decades later when the Indian masses became more resentful of the foreign government because of the humiliation they suffered at their hands, Indian writers felt it necessary to mount an offensive against the British bureaucracy in India. Indian writing became more vocal about injustice, cruelty and exploitation. They painted pathetic conditions in an exaggerated way. These writings were first inspired by Mahatma Gandhi's spirit of liberation from fear and hatred. But the spirit of restraint that sustained them couldn't last long. The partition of Punjab and Bengal ushered in a fissured and flawed freedom—preceded by communal holocaust and bloodier massacres. The heart-rending mass exodus of people across the frontiers became the theme of many novels, for example, Khushwant Singh's *Train to Pakistan* where the East-West differences become an integral part of the texture. Indo-English prose gradually reflected "the dynamic changes and attitudes—social, political, intellectual and material—wrought in the Indian social structure by the contact with the West."[10]

The Indian reality of a conventional, spiritual, unsophisticated Mother India in which extreme poverty is an integral part disturbed the educated Indian, torn between the tensions of tradition and modernity. Indo-English fiction of late has turned to this new quest of East and West in individual probings, following the trends of the novel in the West. The confusion or conflict within the authorial personality finds expression in the East-West encounter of culture-shocks and contrasts, Hindu metaphysics and western pragmatism, racial tension and colonial conflict, European and Indian expatriatism. The drama in the novels emerges from man struggling with nature in its various aspects of environmental hostility, poverty, caste, code tradition and urban cluastrophobia in unhappy combination. Robin White says: "If anything is to distinguish Indian fiction . . . it would be the varied literary attempt to portray this conflict of the contemporary Indian and his past."[11] The Indian's attitude of negation to reality with its multitude of attributes, such as resignation, denial, acceptance, fatalism, withdrawal, passivity, fantasy, world-weariness, moral turpitude, rejection of concern, submission to the past or preference for symbolic or mythic rather than pragmatic action, as preferred by them to the insanity of hopeless opposition, is interpreted as a vision of decay and a philosophy of despair. It is objectified in the philosophic step towards renunciation of illusory attachments, extinction of self and ultimate spiritual fulfilment. The Indian protagonist caught in this web of familiar dualism of tradition versus change, mysticism versus materialism, morality versus free will, is a part of Modern India.

The choice of the English language to write Indian fiction is central to the whole situation of this East-West clash. As Srinivas Iyengar says: "peculiarities of Indian life and experience and speech . . . don't easily admit of translation into English terms."[12] Of special interest therefore is the Indian's creative use of the English language to evoke the genuine currents and nuances of Indian life. R.K. Narayan has successfully created an artistic style out of a lean vocabulary. A handful of writers have also developed an idiosyncratic prose capable of conveying the vital and intractable essence of life. Their prose is alive with things felt and seen and heard, and possesses the richness and rawness of diction, vivacity of speech, circumlocution of thought and subtlety of mystical intonation which orchestrate the Indian experience. Raja Rao has successfully adopted traditional and Puranic modes of narrative. But most writers are handicapped by formal and technical immaturity. They suffer an impulsion to write of urgent inherent subjects and themes overwhelmingly intense in themselves, so that the impulsion of craftsmanship sometimes falls weak by comparison. India must be presented with its contrasts, paradoxes, ambiguities and contradictions of old and new. The magic of the monsoon and the waiting for it in the dusty plains; the strangling jungle, public worship, poverty and the riches of India, its castes and festivals, the interminable ritual of birth, marriage and cremation in a land where non-violence is preached and violence practised, all these have to be interpreted to an audience unfamiliar with it. The English language writer also faces the temptation of interpolating such information into his narrative for the benefit of the foreign reader.

II

This study is aimed at a scrutiny of the writings of Kamala Markandaya and Ruth Prawer Jhabvala to examine their handling of the East-West encounter. Each author is sought to be treated as herself, and the joint examination has been inspired because of similarities in their lives and personalities.

Taking up Kamala Markandaya first, we learn form the WLB biography[13] records that Markandaya attended Madras University. She was deterred from obtaining a degree in history because of her "increasingly strong interest in writing." The war was on and these were crucial years in Anglo-Indian relations. Markandaya lived for a time in a village in South India but set sail for England in 1948 on marrying an Englishman. India has been the country of her birth and upbringing, and England that of her adoption. She returns often to India but her husband and children are English. She herself has become a product of inter-cultural forces. Her personal, social and religious heritage is prone to be touched by her expatriate status. It is not easy to shed the inhibitions and pulls of a parent heritage. It is desirable to examine the extent to which her innate consciousness is affected by her western one to see if the conflict of loyalties finds expression in her writing and the solutions she offers to resolve it.

Ruth Prawer Jhabvala is European by birth, born of Polish parents. She had her upbringing and education in England and came to India only in her adult life because she married an Indian Parsi architect. As she herself admits, "If I hadn't married an Indian, I don't think I would even have come here for I am not attracted—or used not to be attracted—to the things that usually bring people to India."[14] She continues to live in India only because her "strongest human ties are here." Her husband and children are Indian but she herself is not and is even "less so every year." She confesses that India "often proves too strong for European nerves," and can make them irritable like herself. Coming to India after its independence, she has seen and lived with Indians at close quarters and thereby acquired an intimate understanding of their ideas, ideals and various modes of life. Her fiction is based on this knowledge of Indians around her. But she does so with the knowledge of her western consciousness. She observes a very limited class of Indians though. This is only the educated middle-class of Indians around Delhi, chiefly Punjabis, whom as Ved Metha confesses, "the setting of the British sun left . . . with an intellectual contempt for English values, but emotionally . . . too far committed to withdraw . . . condemned to live with a permanent hangover."[15] Jhabvala's own expatriate dilemma finds it difficult to reconcile with the sights and sounds of India: "there comes a point where you have to close up in order to protect yourself." The treatment of the East-West conflict in her novels will be examined in the context of these western influences on the psyche and the lives of Indians living with it, her own expatriate dilemmas of reconciliation, absorption or confrontation, and her ideas for resolving such dilemmas.

It was E.M. Forster who first made suggestions to reconcile relationship between the East and the West. Kamala Markandaya's and Ruth Prawer Jhabvala's writing—because of their personal ties with the East and the West—will also be examined to discover their attempts to diffuse this tension. From their comments it becomes amply evident that they realize that in its present state, the East and the West cannot easily come together. A complete surrender has never been possible nor desirable. A point where they can meet effectively is naturally expected in the stories of these two authors. This study will examine the extent of the author's own temperamental and experiential identification with the phenomenon of cultural schizophrenia, and the extent and possibility of an effective assimilation and their artistic attempts to integrate language with theme.

NOTES

1. See Ved Metha, *Walking the Indian Streets* (London, 1961).
2. *Towards a General Theory of Action,* ed. L. Parsons and E. Shils (Cambridge: Massachusetts, 1951), p. 410.
3. Cora Du Bois, "The Cultural Interplay between East and West," *The East and West Must Meet: A Symposium* (East Lansing: Michigan, 1959), p. 7.
4. Allen J. Greenberger, *The British Image of India* (London, 1969), p. 30.
5. John Masters, *The Night-Runners of Bengal* (New York, 1951).
6. Mrs. Steel, *The Hosts of the Lord,* p. 84.
7. Kamala Markandaya, *Possession* (London, 1963), p. 209.
8. Stephen Hemenway, *The Novel of India* (Calcutta, 1975), II, p. 46.
9. *Loc. cit.*
10. Milton Singar, ed., *Introducing Indian Liberal Education* (Chicago, 1957), p. 142.
11. "Fiction in India," *The Reporter,* Vol. 28, No. 4, Feb. 14,1963, p. 59.
12. K.R. Srinivas Iyengar, *Indian Writing in English* (Delhi, 1984), p. 20.
13. Wilson Library Bulletin, XXVIII, Nov. 63.
14. Ruth Prawer Jhabvala, *How I Became a Holy Mother and Other Stories* (Suffolk, 1976), p. 9.
15. Ved Metha, p. 18.

The Political Encounter

England's relations with India began in 1600 A.D. when a group of London merchants received a charter to trade with the East Indies from Queen Elizabeth I. At first, the trading company restricted itself to trade alone avoiding all attempts at gaining territorial possessions that might have proved ruinous to its trade interests. They built only "factories" along the southern coasts of India till about the end of the century, after which they wanted to establish such "a politic of civil and military power and create and secure such a large revenue to secure both . . . as may be the foundation of a large well-grounded sure English dominion in India for all times to come."[1] They worked their political ambitions insidiously until entering into the "very bone and marrow"[2] and conquered India. The prevailing political condition with the disintegration of Mughal rule and the feuding principalities ensured Robert Clive's victory in the battle of Plassey in 1757, establishing the dominance of the English over the political life of Bengal—gateway to the rest of northern India. Later, Warren Hastings extended "the influence of the British nation to every part of India not too remote from their possessions, without enlarging the circle of their defence or involving them in hazardous or indefinite engagement."[3] The defeat of British arms and influence at Saratoga in 1777, in the American War of Independence inspired them to retrieve their national honour in India. Their consolidation of power and authority saw far-reaching changes. India was then "a vast sub-continent, a Europe in itself" and Hastings engaged in preserving British dominion from Indian assault. Lord Cornwallis further consolidated that power by Europeanizing the services, filling the upper and middle cadres of the revenue, judicial and commercial branches with Europeans alone.

The country was divided into districts and the collector made responsible for revenue collection through the zamindars who acquired enhanced power over the peasant in this English system of landlordism. The Rule of Law, hitherto unknown in India, was introduced. A judge administered that law while a police force maintained law and order.

Lord Wellesley arrived under strict injunction to "keep the peace, not to meddle with the Indian rulers."[4] To keep the English Company supreme in India he introduced the Subsidiary Alliance of the Indian states which assumed the English power as being dominant. Under the treaty, native states surrendered their external relations to the Company and negotiated with other states, through the Company. For this, a British Resident was appointed to each state. No other foreigner was allowed in residence in the state and an army commanded by British officers was maintained by the state. The system increased the English military strength in the native states without adding to their own financial burden and added strategic territories to the Company's dominions. These "Trojan horse tactics" were steps in empire building and assured the fidelity of the native rulers who were made to live in "abject dependence upon the will of the British agency at their various courts."[5]

Lord Dalhousie cowed the native princes further by introducing the Doctrine of Lapse which made infructuous the Hindu practice of adopting an heir. The throne could come by an adopted son only when sanctioned by the paramount power and not as a rule. It hurt the religious sentiments of the people while the native rulers lived in fear of their territories being confiscated by the British.

Sir John Malcolm opines "that the tranquillity . . . security of our own vast oriental possessions is involved in the preservation of native principalities . . . dependent on us for protection."[6] Apart from the direct benefits that the English derived from the alliance, the states acted as "cess-pits into which the accumulating miseries of the rest of India could seep . . . and prey on each other." The concentration of power without responsibility in the Residents wrought corruption and favouritism.

The English rule so long as it provided "merely a framework of security beneath which traditional society could continue"[7] was appreciated and respected for its orderliness. Later when the Evangelicals and the Radicals believing passionately in the superiority of the western world interfered with custom and society, British rule became "remote and olympian."[8] Indians found no part of it. Trade moved in a restricted way and inter-town commerce that had flourished in the Mughal days came to a standstill. A mighty bureaucracy was created on the characteristics defined by Max Weber functioning according to the established Rule of Law.[9]

Lord William Bentinck was "the pilot mainly responsible for trimming the sails of the British-Indian state to the winds of change."[10] He was "a reforming Mughal," introducing West to East in administrative affairs, creating two new grades of Indian judges, the first real break-away from the Cornwallis system of European monopoly in higher office. But the English education awoke the Indians to the dignity of man and the need for individual liberty. It can therefore be justifiably said that "national feeling did not germinate of its own accord in the soil of India; rather it was an exotic growth implanted by foreign hands and influences."[11]

Indians who had been encouraged to take English education were denied higher positions reserved strictly for Englishmen, such discrimination and denial of facilities and advantages of full-fledged citizens of the country were aggravated by the numerous hurdles placed in their way of taking the civil services examinations, held only in English and based on a syllabus that an English education in India did not meet. The civil services was the highest-paid and most prestigious service in the world. But Indians could only go on to clerical jobs. Lack of capital and caste restrictions kept them away from business as "the trade of the colonials was permissible only so far as it seemed consistent with the economic interest" of England.[12]

In 1857 there was a mutiny of sepoys on the use of greased cartridges that went against the old culture. It sparked "a national and holy war waged with the object of securing freedom from English bondage."[13] As a result, what had been the Company's dominions were brought directly under the Crown. The mutiny also roused and increased racial ill-will between the two peoples. The war had been fought with great ferocity on both sides and the reprisals were savage. The Indian soldier was divided between strong feelings of loyalty and religion and it found manifestation in the extremity of outward action. The British saw themselves threatened with destruction and withdrew into their shell of vanity not associating with the natives. An enduring estrangement between the two races grew, till the relationship became increasingly one of master and slave. Native princes had not sided with the insurgents and Lord Canning gratefully acknowledged these "breakwaters in the storm which would have swept over us in one great wave."[14] After 1857, these "essential pillars of the British Raj" were integrated into the Indian empire of Queen Victoria with a personal relationship with the monarch. The Governor-General was given the added honorific of Viceroy and the legislative council was reorganized to include a few aristocratic Indians, landed gentry and native princes. The new westernized middle classes were however neglected and began to echo the war-cry of the Americans of "no taxation without representation." For the first time in India's history this English-educated elite had a common language, a common idea and common attitudes. Their exclusion from higher office, the denial of equality with the Europeans in the judicial service despite the Ilbert Bill, brought them together in the common forum of the Indian National Congress where they voiced their political opinion. The district officials considered such men seditious and viewed them with suspicion. Curzon's appointment was therefore at first hailed by the Indians because of his impartiality; but the extravagance at the Delhi Durbar of 1903 and later the Universities Act was taken by the educated elite "as bureaucratic interference and a calculated attack on the new nationalism."[15]

The First World War formed a watershed in modern Indian development. The princes responded with enthusiasm to their recent largesse with men and money. The middle classes in general hoped for a redressal when every proposal of theirs was met with an "after the war." But when the war prolonged, Congress took the initiative and there began a series of revolutions, led by Mahatma Gandhi, to protest in the traditional Indian method of a *hartal.* The response to the *hartal* was enthusiastic and encompassed even women in their thousands. Businessmen came forth without counting the cost or consequences, nor was labour daunted by the prospect of spending foodless days. At one such protest-meeting in the Jallianwala Bagh at Amritsar, General Dyer chose to fire on a defenceless crowd without warning. Racial bitterness was now added to the general discontent and it was only Gandhi's influence that contained large-scale violence. But when Dyer's action was appreciated by the House of Lords, even Gandhi who had advocated cooperation with the British, withdrew all support to "this Satanic government." A non-cooperation movement was launched which put the government under visible strain. Gandhi, dressed in homespun *dhoti* and *shawl*, identified with the masses. He fought for the rights of man not only with the British and South Africans but also with the caste Hindus and worked for communal unity.

The Congress demanded complete independence when the parliament was reappointed with an all-British membership. Gandhi was invited to the Round Table Conference in 1931. It broke down and led to more agitations and repressions. The "'little man' in the Palace with no proper clothes and bare knees,"[16] whom His Majesty could not stomach at tea in the Buckingham Palace, was seen as "the messiah of his countrymen"[17] by millions of English people who had no sympathy with their rulers on the Indian question. In 1935 the federal principle was adopted including the princes who had direct treaty with the Crown.

Soon came the Second World War which was none of India's business till the entry of Japan brought the War to India's doorstep and made it an intimate concern. If the political situation had been clearer the Indian attitude may have been more positive. In August 1942 the demand for the withdrawal of the British from India was effected. The police and magistrates were given "unbridled powers to do whatever they chose"[18] and they arrested several Congress personalities and put them in prisons in different parts of the country. The sudden removal of the nation's leaders provoked deep resentment among the masses who reacted with greater fury and the government repressed with equal vigour.

The English could never conceive of India as one nation. The conflict arose out of their reluctance to respect India's sovereignty. India was indeed the "most truly bright and precious gem in the crown of the Queen." India had raised the power, resources and wealth of that small island. They did not want to give it up to untrained and agitating politicians. India they felt would never survive the Raj but it did, to become independent in August 1947. The native states were given the option to merge with either India or the truncated Muslim-dominated Pakistan, and that wrought a change in their hitherto independent status. Most of the states merged with India and in the new socialist democracy were left with only a few princely privileges.

Indian-English political relationship has been evaluated variously by Indo-English writers. Indian writing in English is so inextricably linked with these political developments that even R.K. Narayan, who fears politics as a Western nemesis, could not completely ignore what he thought had put the West in a muddle. His Malgudi was affected by the changes wrought by the British impact.

Kamala Markandaya and Ruth Prawer Jhabvala survey this political phenomenon as the cause for a breakdown in personal relationship. They also enquire into its catalyst character as it changed man's attitudes and ideologies or shaped their destinies.

II

Kamala Markandaya has a generally patriotic tone when handling political confrontation between Britain and India. Without taking sides she vehemently decries the role of the British as rulers and the political mess India has landed itself in. Her attitude finds expression in the chararcter of Roshan Merchant in her novel *Some Inner Fury*[19] who says that the English were insufferable as overlords but humane, civilized and charming as individuals. Political dichotomy takes three forms in her novels: firstly, there is a mingling of political history with fiction; secondly, the impact of the western political system which was not always in consonance with Indian lives, and finally, the breakdown of personal relations because of political wranglings.

Mingling political history with fiction is not new to Indian writing in English. From its very beginning, political and historical events of importance have been woven into fiction. Some such novels are *History of a Bengal Raiyat* by Lal Behari Dey in 1874, *The Young Zamindar* by Sochee Chunder Dutt in 1885, and *Sanjogita* by R.K. Sinha in 1903. Later there were novels that reflected India's political attitude at the beginning of the Indian National Congress like *The Prince of Destiny* by Sarath Kumar Ghose and *Hindupore* by Sidha Mohan Mitra in 1909. Disillusionment with the British and the advent of Gandhi formed the background of stories like *Murugan the Tiller* by K.S. Venkatramani in 1927 and *Kandan the Patriot* in 1932. Later there was Mulk Raj Anand's *Untouchable* indirectly dealing with the national movement. K. Nagarjan's *Athawar House*, K.A. Abbas's *Tomorrow is Ours*, Raja Rao's *Kanthapura* are also aspects of the freedom struggle.

Markandaya mingles political history with fiction in her second novel *Some Inner Fury* in which political conflict becomes the core of the plot. Her sense of history, which she had been studying, is carefully woven into the environment in which Mira's and Richard's love goes awry. Taking the aberrations of Gandhi's non-violence movement she traces the insurmountables that separate Mira and Richard. Mira belongs to a rich, sophisticated family that has been admitted into the British social circle. Her own brother Kit has obtained his education abroad and has successfully competed into the Indian Civil Service. Juxtaposed is her foster-brother Govind who gives up his education mid-way and ranges himself with the agitators for freedom. He leaves home and is rumoured to have joined a group of violent agitators, though very little is known of his activities. It is Kit who brings home Richard Marlowe, the young army officer whom he has met on the ship. The young Mira feels the first flush of romance as she falls in love with the

Englishman. Richard soon goes away but as luck would have it, Mira unknown to herself follows him to that same place, which she goes to for a short holiday with her brother Kit and sister-in-law Premala. She is surprised to meet Roshan Merchant, another of Kit's sophisticated, English-educated friends who had been a daring socialite, now in home-spun cotton publishing a paper for the nationalist movement. Roshan persuades Mira to join her paper and in the course of her journalistic duties she is brought once more to Richard, the Governor's ADC. Mira is accompanied by Richard the ADC to a project sponsored by the British Government which Mira is reporting. Mira like all Indians is sceptic of the Government's welfare project and remarks: "I hear Her Excellency's given the land." Richard, conscious of the power and authority of the crown now under question in India, retorts: "Does it matter . . . who granted it?" Mira, fiercely patriotic: "To those most concerned, no. To everyone else?" Richard relents non-committally but Mira remarks: "In other countries, in other times perhaps not; but here in India, in the middle of war and civil war?" Richard is suddenly aware of a serious difference between them and says quickly, "Has it infected you too—all this 'your people' and 'my people'?" (138)

Markandaya weaves strands of political events into Mira's narrative which co-ordinate the aspect of time in this novel. With the declaration of the Second World War in Europe in 1939 the English in India are filled with "shadows and fears and a sense of the tragic fury gathering across the seas." (108) The Indians, concerned only with their own freedom, are "aware of that other storm impending in the country." The agitation reaches a crescendo in the Quit India Movement of 1942 which seems to fence in the romantic young lovers. "The creeping hostility" around Richard is evident in the deathly silence of the *hartal* that has gripped the town to which they return from their holiday. Banners ask men like him to go away, they are unwanted; a bottle of acid hurled at him barely misses him. Mira in her love shields him with her Indian presence but Richard wonders, "Is it safer for me if we're together?" The political drama of 1942 is thus authenticated into their personal drama.

In a graphic description Markandaya captures the glory of the British rule in India. Mira, waltzing at a ball in the Government House is struck by the incongruities of the heavy gilt-framed portraits "of governors and viceroys, paintings of battles and surrenders, Clive and Hastings, Plassey and Seringapatnam—British faces, Indian history—circling and circling around." (207) But an hour later after an anti-British demonstration at the Government House when Mira and Kit rush to the missionary Hickey's school in search of Premala who helped there with the children, the description of the burning school becomes symbolic of the blood-stained annihilation of British rule in India: "The framework began to buckle, the iron-girders melting and supple, were swaying back and forth, in and out, tirelessly until the rivets gave in. For a moment the girders hung motionless; then slowly gathering force, they fell, twisting, writhing, white hot-limbs that lashed and coiled and clung to each other and so in this last furious shapeless embrace dipped closer and closer to that violet bed of fire." (217) Kit is killed in the violence at the school, Premala is burnt inside the school building and Govind is arrested for the incident. At his trial, the English judge accepts the evidence of the missionary Hickey, as against that of the Indians and Mira realizes "the terrible power of the English." She is filled with hatred for them and knows she must leave Richard. Being an Englishman he was with his countrymen just as she was with her country—"there was no other way, the forces that pulled us apart were too strong." (285)

In an article entitled "On Images," Kamala Markandaya expands on the thought that literature can play a constructive role by laying "bare the very anatomy of destruction and so force a halt."[20] In this book she has induced in her reader a sense of horror at the evil of violence. When the terror of the situation is recognized by mankind, can there be redressal? Political violence has become Mira's cruel fate "what matter to the world, if here and there a man should fall, or a head or a heart should break." (285-86)

In her third novel *A Silence of Desire*,[21] political history finds only an occasional reverberation. Chari, who heads Dandekar's office, had been an I.C.S. officer. But he resigned his service when it went against his conscience to work on for a government he didn't approve of. "After a further long period of waiting he joined the Congress party. . . . A good deal of the next decade . . . he spent in gaol. . . . When independence came these gaol sentences stood him in good stead, nicely balancing the prejudice in an intensely Indian India against his former British liaison." (22)

Her fourth novel *Possession* is really a "microcosmic rendering of England's possession of India."[22] Lady Caroline Bell who visits India in 1949 was "descended from a long line of men who had ruled India in the days of the British Raj." (9) Her father had been Resident to the erstwhile prince, Jumbo, and it is at his dinner that Caroline meets the Indian writer Anasuya who gives us their story. Caroline and Anasuya set off in search of arak. Caroline finds a young shepherd painting crudely the cave-walls outside this South Indian village. She sees in him potential material gains and without caring for any one's feelings is able to take him away for a sum of money. Caroline holds Valmiki as tenaciously as we are informed England did India—the extended metaphor almost marring the symbolical effects of the novel. Valmiki has been whisked away in body but his spirit remains in India and for a long time he is unable to produce any work in English. Caroline treats him as a business proposition—sometimes pandering to his whims and fancies, often being irritated by them. Valmiki is grateful to her for her patronage, something he never got at home, but her hold over him is also annoying to him. They share, we are told, "a sort of love-hate relationship . . . like the kind Britain and India used to have." (69) The Englishmen in England had been sympathetic to India's cause and Gandhi's visit had made an indelible impression on their hearts. Caroline's English housekeeper Mrs. Peabody recalls Gandhi's visit to London when she had been a little girl, "'he was a lad, he,' she would say with the chuckle that came into her voice. Whenever she spoke of him, her eyes kindling with the memory of whatever I was that had captivated her. 'Always smiling, and a word for everyone and the kids splitting their sides with his jokes and that' . . . and then with reverence, 'He was a gentleman, no clothes and all'." (79)

In *A Handful of Rice*,[23] political history is alive in the ruins and monuments of foreign dominance. Ravi, the vagabond hero, identifies them for his young wife Nalini when he takes her on a tour of the city. His limited English learning has informed him that the Portuguese had first come to San Thome or that the British Tommies came storming down from St. Thomas Mount to maraud and rape. Nalini agrees that there had been bad times when women had gone in great fear of this swaggering lusting Tommies. But foreigners have come and gone in India's history but "we remain, we Indians that is all that matters." (133)

The Nowhere Man[24] documents racial prejudices that are being spearheaded in recent political history, in England. Srinivas is an Indian expatriate who had left India with his wife Vasantha at the height of the freedom struggle, to escape being arrested for underground activities against the British rule in India. Their families had been opposed to British arrogance in India. Srinivas's mother had been angered by the number of lives lost in the Jallianwala tragedy, even if it had been a retaliatory step. That "a hundred Indians" should be killed for each Britain was "their scale, the scale by which they value themselves and against which we are measured. That is what we are up against; not their greed or their anger, nor land hunger, nor the need to trade; but their arrogance the mentality that produces such policies and acts." (122) Srinivas and his friend Abdul Zanzibari from Madagascar are filled with memories—one of India, the other of Africa, of flags that had followed the spice trade and the crimes committed in their name. Ironically, they both set up a business in spices in England. They were both damaged badly by the workings of empire and carried the hurt within them. Srinivas's sons are born and brought up in England. One of them, Seshu, even joins the British forces and is killed by a German shell. The heart-broken Vasantha wants to "return to our country. There is no reason now that India is free, why we should not." (38) Racialism of a more violent kind is spreading its tentacles in England as more and more whites find themselves deprived of a living. The Asians are conscious about the ill-will let loose on them. Once again the author produces a cathartic effect by heightening Srinivas's tragic existence.

In *Two Virgins*,[25] the scene shifts once more to India. Political history is recounted in the story of Appa's family in a post-Independent village. It is chiefly in the diatribe of the older generation against the British rule in India that history is recalled. Appa had been "a fighter for freedom" but the British called him a terrorist. He had printed leaflets on the freedom struggle and stuffed his ancestral home with them; but it was burnt down when the British police discovered it. After the struggle, when India gained independence, Appa was left without any possession or job till the government rewarded him for his actions with a plot of not very arable land. There were others, like Appa's compatriot, Rangu, who had not lived to see India free but had fought even more fiercely for it and suffered more grievously at the hands of the British police. The British before leaving had made sure to divide the people so that India was partitioned amidst the holocaust of riots. Now India was free and the people had the vote to change things. There is too much of pontification on Britain's political role in India; their aloofness from the people they ruled which reflected in a scanty respect for the country's customs. There is a harping on the crippling of home industry in the face of imposition of British-manufactured goods. Like *Possession,* this novel too suffers from a repetition of the theme of Britain's overlordship. In fact much of the book is a treatise on that issue alone—a criticism of their role in India and occasionally an invective against society in general. Political history does not in any way contribute to the story's plot or have any significant bearing on it.

Of all her novels, *The Golden Honeycomb*[26] borrows most extensively of India's political history vis-a-vis the English. Unlike the previous book it is not a mere documentation of history; woven into the saga of a native princely family are political events that shaped their lives. The novel begins with the deposition of a native ruler who had the temerity to defy the English. The people are at pains to find a suitable incumbent and must abide by social custom in selecting one of a suitable caste. The Kshatriya lad is chosen to become Bawajiraj I and he reconciles himself to a secondary role in the matters of state that are really handled by the British Resident. His son Bawajiraj II is taken care of by the British from his very birth. Markandaya chronicles the ways and means the British adopted to create this special class of Indians alienated from the rest of their countrymen. His education was planned to make him a loyal subject of the British Crown, "convinced of the soundness and moral integrity of the Empire." He was moulded into a perfect British stooge to whom the Durbar in Delhi was "a most important affair." He took pride in entertaining the British authorities to shoots and hunts and is seriously troubled by the delay in the delivery of his guns when the Kaiser Bill is affected. The First World War drew from him a very enthusiastic response in terms of men and money. He even volunteers his own services but his consort Mohini will not allow their son Rabi to enlist. Bawajiraj II is aware that Rabi's ascendancy to the throne depends on the Viceroy's opinion because of his illegitimate status and he does everything to appease the English. Bawajiraj II is a prototype of the native prince. But his mistress Mohini is more earthy and Indian. She ensures that Rabi learns about his country as well. It is Rabi's visit to Bombay that awakens him. Through the plight of the textile mill-workers he becomes aware of the problems of India. His visit to the Durbar also awakens him to the role played by the native princes. He is caught in the fervour of nationalism and is determined that "insupportable levies and treaties must be rescinded" for which they would "continue the struggle to that end." He is equally furious that "rajahs and nawabs have rent the country apart for a century and more and in the process traders and soldiers of fortune have been elevated into emperors." The Indian people had begun to repair the damage and Rabi is on their side.

British India is caught up in the cry for freedom while the native states are still outside this turmoil. The Dewan of Devapur had judiciously kept himself away from the activities of British India but his daughter and son-in-law are arrested for participating in freedom meetings and lodged in British jails. There was a strength of purpose in the cause of freedom that united all and sundry. The political events in this book bring about a change in Rabi's character. He becomes purposeful, determined. The change is not abrupt but gradual as he is brought face to face with real events that move him to a decision.

Political overlordship provided the English the prerogative to impose new systems on India which were not always in consonance with the spirit of India and crippled its economy.

In her first novel *Nectar in a Sieve*[27] the semi-literate peasant woman Rukmani and her husband Nathan are victims of the system of landlordism, introduced by the English. As tenant farmers, they go through the trials and tribulations of paying land rent, during even famine and flood to the absentee landlord and what is worse never owning the land. At a time when "white men have power" (52) there is an apathetic neglect of governmental aid. Instead of improving agricultural yields, industry comes in the form of a tannery to upset the agrarian equilibrium which also signifies a symbolic break with the traditional peace of the land. The tannery brings with it the filthy commerce of a town. The death of Rukmani's son in the trouble at the tannery is compensated with money. Her sons clamour for more money to eat their fill. Rukmani is soon deprived of the land and driven to seek out another son in the city. She never finds him and is reduced to the state of a beggar with all her meagre belongings stolen. Finally, thrown upon the resources of the city-urchin Puli, Rukmani and Nathan take to the arduous task, breaking stones in the quarry. Nathan is so shattered by the loss of his self-respect, his state of near-beggary and poor nourishment that he dies a broken man. Rukmani, reconciled to the change, returns with Puli to her native village.

In *Some Inner Fury*, Kit, educated abroad and competing into the civil service, is also alienated from the grim realities of India's problems. To Premala's consternation, he is anglicized like the English officers. His foster-brother Govind is wedded to India's cause which makes him sympathetic to Premala.

In *A Silence of Desire*, Dandekar with his English education has procured a clerical job in a Government office. In post-independence India he often discusses in his office that the English built the roads, railways and bridges in India for their own convenience. Dandekar's education sets him in conflict with the beliefs of his older traditional thinking. He believes that only medical assistance can be his wife Sarojini's cure for her tumour.

In *Possession,* Caroline is "well born, really rich in the English way with landed estates and money in sterling," (9) a class they strove to raise in India which with its English education would be Indian only in blood. This class of erstwhile princes like Jumbo had held the English ruling class in thrall. After independence he laments that in the new socialist democracy "princes are two per paise, fighting Congress wallahs for the public posts . . . the power and the influence . . . is among the representatives of the people." (165) But when they had counted, there had been the regalia of office which became symbolic of India to the English who never met any other Indian. In independent India, the poor Indian accustomed to the princes's old authority and splendour still expects to see him in the same finery. If Jumbo is willing to forsake that finery he will not tolerate its being donned by the young painter Valmiki either, as he was not entitled to it by birth. The change has been difficult for the princes. Used to associating only with the English ruling classes they can be seen commuting "between continent and continent . . . they can't face India." Anasuya, by contrast, is educated but not elitist and finds it easy to return, "simply because . . . I can always come back here, feel at home with my own family and be received by people like you," (92) she tells Jumbo.

That the English as rulers had been aloof is borne out by the village headman. Before independence "they did not care if we had no water. Or perhaps they did not know our need of it." (167) But after freedom having been given the power to vote "three wells have been dug in the village in six months . . . one with English money, one with American, third the Russians dug themselves." (167) India was severely handicapped by its years of submission and was "staggering along behind everyone else . . . at last getting there, even if those centuries of ferocious paternalism had affected her growth as that she walked like an uncertain toddler instead of the adult she now was." (162)

A Handful of Rice is what the vagabond Ravi is striving for in the city. K.R. Srinivas Iyengar draws attention to the fact that Ravi's predicament can only be understood after a knowledge of "the spiralling grain prices in India. Bad monsoons have caused havoc in the lives of millions and bad governments have proved incapable of effectively holding the price line."[21] The ideals of achieving freedom died with getting the English out in body though the imperious spirit lingered on. The fusion of an Indian government with a Western mind proved disastrous. Ravi is a victim of this English nemesis. He is one of the poorly English-educated who flock to the city looking for white-collar jobs. His father, a poor peasant, had been proud of and insisted on this learning "as a key to the power of earning which was the broad base of a man's pride." (26-27) But the key opened no magical doors. Contrarily, it closed them for him. The city was full of graduates looking for employment amongst whom he stood with the little chance of his meagre education. It had, on the other hand, taken away his "ability to work with his hands except in an amateur capacity." (26-27) At home in the village, things were no better for tenant farmers. The old tailor Apu, into whose house Ravi had broken into in a state of drunkenness, was adept at his trade and took pride in his work. He had built up a large clientele and could successfully make both ends meet. Ravi too was capable of hard work but his heart was not in being a tradesman. He was more sensitive to the class-structure and wanted to get into that ruling class by fair means or foul. He sees the corrupt ways in which money has been accrued to spell respectability—Damodar's profiteering ways; in being underpaid by the "memsahibs," in smuggling foreign goods when they had been boycotted during the freedom struggle. The appetites of those who felt that "indefinable something that set them above the common herd was whetted." The class-structure of the rich and the poor has taken firm root and disparities widen with the poor being deprived of basic essentials of food and proper medical care and housing so that Ravi cries out in despair, "the same, same class, same money, even coming from different countries, makes no difference compared to that. It's the sameness that makes them stick together." (153)

The Coffer Dams[29] is a story about the time in post-independent India when "the country was full of foreigners . . . all of them eager in greater or lesser degree, to gain a foothold in an expanding sub-continent of vast commercial potential." (10) The building of these dams in hilly Karnataka is bagged by a firm of English technologists in which Indian engineers and tribal labourers also participate. The English make a frenetic bid to complete the dam according to their stringent planning, making no leeway even for unpredictable weather conditions. Accidents occur; the men lay off work on account of it and are not paid. The tribals had no natural instinct for money or commerce but now being used to it they were becoming "as money-minded as you foreigners are." According to the tribal chief money had no use for these men except for that rubbish they buy from the camp-shop like tin cans, cardboard boots and scented pig's grease for their hair. The needs of food could easily be met with what they could get from the jungle and they might have been spared this anguish.

There were other delays like the misplacement of essential equipment. The unwieldy bureaucracy set up by the English in India was inefficient and bossy. Not properly educated either, there were numerous bunglings and gross errors. Corruption became rampant because of their authority without responsibility, an example of which could be seen in the poor construction of quarters whose "walls bulged, roofs leaked, doors warped and rattled in their frames."

In *Two Virgins*, there is no work for Appa to do in the restructuring of a new India. He sits and blames all the present-day ills on British subjugation, like the inefficient sewerage system which they had not organized in their 200-year rule. He insisted that they had started the opium trade to line their own pockets. But when it came to educating his favourite daughter Lalitha, he chose to send her to the English school run by Miss Mendoza for a tidy fee because of the opportunities it afforded.

The Golden Honeycomb is a period novel in which there is no scope to touch on British influences that survived the Raj.

It is really the third dimension of this political confrontation, the breakdown of personal relations, that Markandaya is chiefly concerned about.

In *Nectar in a Sieve*, Rukmani sought Dr. Kenny's medical assistance which helped her bear a son but she did not wish her husband to know "I was putting myself in the hands of a foreigner." He was "a friend to her father's house," her own "benefactor," but because of being English he was dubbed as being one with the rulers and oppressors. Rukmani therefore meets Kenny furtively because she "was sure Nathan would not like his wife or his daughter going to a whiteman, a foreigner."

In *Some Inner Fury*, this diseased political structure poisons every aspect of potential East-West kinship. Mira experiences an ardent, honest, guileless love in the arms of Richard but it is a cursed relationship. They become representatives of their two nations—one ruled, the other ruler. Ironically, Mira belongs to a class that shares social relations with the English but there were dangers in loving an Englishman at such a time: "The conventions of his caste were no less rigid than mine; he came of a race which had acquired an empire, to which the people at home were largely indifferent and of which the people on the spot were largely ignorant." (159) Their relationship undergoes a change when caught in the vortex of the Quit India movement. Mira confesses: "I knew now that the silence of these streets enfolded me too, I was a part of it, it no longer repudiated me and from within its invisible envelope, do what I could, there was no easy reaching out to those who stood outside." (159) Richard is on that outside. He feels terrible to feel unwanted, to be hated. He was one of the Englishmen against whom this ire had been let loose: "You belong to one side, if you don't belong to the other. It's as simple as that, even children understand it. And in between? There is no in between. You have shown your badge, you have taken your stance." (218)

In *A Silence of Desire*, Dandekar's colleagues recall that the English bureaucrats had prophesied ineptitude. muddle and disaster after they left and had firmly believed that the Indians were incapable of carrying on with the grave institutions they had taken pains to set up. Such remarks smacked of the British superiority which alienated them from their Indian colleagues.

In *Possession*, Caroline's possessive hold over Valmiki is resentful to him. Anasuya the writer likens this "forcible possessing" as establishing nothing "as clearly as that there could be no reasonable relationship—merely a straddling of one stronger by another with little out of it for either." (69) Anasuya's own relations with Caroline suffer on account of her imperious nature, inherited from the political situation. Caroline would like to dismiss it as "a classic ailment" one which England and India never understood. But Anasuya belongs to a free India and often retorts. There is a mutual inclination "to prick faults and probe vulnerabilities that lay like a legacy in the blood from the long opposition of her line to mine." (133) Anasuya, in her frequent visits to London, finds that the English people in their own island home were warm and cold in turn.

In *A Handful of Rice*, Ravi's ire against the English is only because they are his customers who behave in a high-handed manner; make him use the backstairs, underpay him and treat him as if he were a block of wood. They are cold and aloof because of their superior status. In *The Coffer Dams*, when British technologists and Indian engineers work together, each side carries memories of a colonial past. Clinton had served in several colonies and was generally disdainful of the natives. Krishnan "had lived through and been soured by imperial insolence"; he was acutely sensitive to India's subordinate role, first politically and now technically and mistook all friendliness for compassion. He saw Clinton and his team "brush us off like flies . . . hurt and insult us like splinters under his skin; despise us because they are experts and we are just beginning." (19) He accused them in his mind of that neglect which barred them from such knowledge. Clinton's wife Helen who knew little of this political history preferred a hand of friendship but Krishnan could not grasp it. If she thought Indians subservient, Krishnan blamed it to years of slavery that had accustomed them to being done out of their rights. Only Mackendricks was able to trace this unfriendliness to "the noxious emotional cauldron that Britain the ruler and India the ruled had kept on the boil throughout the term of an imposed overlordship to the humiliation of being an underdeveloped pauper nation." (43) Those like Millie Rawlings who had had past experience of a colonial life saw only one relationship between colonists and natives—that of "overseer and serf." No decent relations could be had between them. Gopal Rao the young engineer was bullied about the loans that an underdeveloped India never repaid to the countries of the West. Self-respect hurt, he retorts "you also have taken from others" and goes on to list the Elgin marbles and Koh-i-noor for which they never paid. Relations are never cordial because of the political wranglings.

In *The Nowhere Man*, racial animosity is bred out of a different political background. The younger generation in England wish to stem the inflow of coloured immigrants. Fred-Fletcher spearheads this anti-coloured agitation in Srinivas's neighbourhood of Ashcroft Avenue. He is even violent in his efforts to reject Srinivas who has lived amicably with the English for long years: "Outraged eyeball challenged eyeball, glazing over with rejection." (181) But there was still hope in liberals like Mrs. Pickering with whom Srinivas is able to strike up a fruitful relationship.

In *Two Virgins*, Appa is a relic of the freedom movement who has had unpleasant relations with the British government. Amma and Aunt Alamelu are therefore also opposed to it. What does not meet with Amma's approval is dumped on the Europeans. Appa however is more restrained and opines, "One imbibes what is bad in the West as well as what is good . . . there are no national frontiers." (113)

The Golden Honeycomb traces in a less vivid way the difficulties of a personal relation against political animosities. The Dewan of Devapur and the British Agent could have met as equals, both being capable men of learning but "the dominant subservient roles written into and essential for the survival of Empire . . . preclude such a meeting." (25) There were attempts at comaraderie and Sir Arthur even considers "this . . . one's country too, bone of one's bone not to mention certain incursions of the spirit," but there were gaps and fences too, to maintain a separate and distinct identity. The Dewan commends the British for their impeccable organization and unparalleled administration. Sir Arthur even helps to get the Dewan's daughter and son-in-law out of the prison in British India. But when Sophie, Sir Arthur's daughter, and Rabi the illegitimate son of Bawajiraj II discover themselves in love, that love is doomed by the prejudices of the ruling nation and the ruled. Sophie's mother, Lady Copeland, is haunted by the memories of her grandfather being stabbed to death by one of his own soldiers in the Mutiny of 1857 and her grandmother who had just nearly escaped multiple rape. Her grandmother had warned against all Indians being savages: "Never trust one. Not one. Even." Lady Copeland therefore is convinced that to love India, "the treacherous Mata Hari" would only result in a trial of ruin and disaster. Sophie's love becomes unnecessarily complicated. Rabi knows, "It's an inherited situation bound to throw up endless problems" because of being "bred by haughty seizures of territory." (443)

There is no dark pessimism in highlighting this confrontation but optimism that the new can learn from the old to forgive and forget and live together in a spirit of reconciliation. Unnecessary pain and anguish can be overcome in the larger interests of humanity.

III

In Ruth Prawer Jhabvala, political confrontation between the East and the West runs a different course. Polish by birth, English by upbringing and Indian only by marriage, Jhabvala lacks Markandaya's natural zeal for India's freedom struggle. She does not need the other's patriotism either, as far as India is concerned. Jhabvala on her own admission is not Indian but having chosen to write about people of North India, particularly Delhi, she cannot ignore the considerable influences of the Raj on these people, the influences which they carried with them into a free India. Besides, their destinies were also shaped by political events which over-ran their lives. Delhi was swarmed by refugees from a partitioned Punjab when India attained freedom and was truncated into a

Muslim-dominated Pakistan. Survivors of that holocaust had lost well-nigh everything and were engaged in building their fortunes anew in Delhi. The ways and means they adopted provide her the opportunity to assess the prevailing political conditions in a free India. She juxtaposes these with the political ideologies that swayed the men of the freedom struggle. Political confrontation between the East and the West in her novels may be categorized accordingly. Firstly the occasional dippings into political history. Secondly the inept administration that suffers a hangover of the Raj.

In *To Whom She Will*,[30] Amrita is the daughter of the late Nirad Chakravarty, a political idealist and freedom fighter. He has been called to the Bar in England and from his photographs he could be seen to have been "very thin and earnest in a tight-fitting European suit." (23) But on returning to India, like Markandaya's Roshan Merchant in *Some Inner Fury*, Nirad Chakravarty gave up all to join the freedom movement. As his widow Radha said, "those times were quite different. Then it was an honour to be poor and have nothing." And Nirad Chakravarty took to wearing white Khadi clothes and was often with Congress personalities including Gandhi himself. Like them he had gone to prison and a picture of his taken in 1944 (two years after the upsurge of the freedom movement of 1942) show him overshadowed by death. Jhabvala is not very clear about the freedom movement so that she confines herself to these fringes. The family of Hari Sahni, Amrita's colleague at the All India Radio and the man she fancies herself in love with, are "Punjabi Hindus who in 1947, at the time of partition, had had to leave their native Lahore which was incorporated into Pakistan and fly to Delhi." (43) Like all other refugees they had lost their valuables, houses and business. The accounts of both these instances are perfunctory but arise out of political history.

The next novel, *The Nature of Passion*,[31] is also about the Punjabi refugee family of Lala Narayan Dass Verma who is set to making good for himself in Delhi by fair means or foul.

Esmond in India[32] traces the fortunes of the family of Ram Nath, a political idealist, and Har Dayal, a political opportunist. Ram Nath, like Nirad Chakravarty of the first book, had obtained an education abroad and been very gay and extravagant like an English nobleman. But on returning to India he gave up all to join the Congress. His sister Uma and her husband had also donated their magnificent, richly furnished house for party work. Much of their property was forfeited by the Government in the years between 1918 and 1947 and the rest was spent recklessly in the course of campaigns and voluntary work. The house had been "full of people and activity, there had been meetings and so much talk and business." Youngmen out of college came to help with office work and typing, earnest, enthusiastic, spending all their time here, so that the house became a centre for the lives and activities of many people. Uma reminisced about that time in "20 or 21" when Ram Nath came out of jail and "everybody" came to welcome him and they had cooked for a large number of people. But before anyone could eat, the police came to rearrest him so that he returned to jail. At another time Uma had sat on Ram Nath's papers feigning labour-pains when the police came to ransack and raid the house. But Uma feels it was all worth it "for Our Country, for Our Cause" and everyone was involved in it. But there had also been men like Har Dayal who was "a scholar of leisure, a gentleman respected and respectable with several friends in British official circles." (92)

In *Get Ready for Battle*,[33] Vishnu remembers that in his childhood he had gone to political meetings with his mother, taken part in demonstrations, processions and communal spinning. Mass-meetings were addressed by the white-capped Congress leaders. In every novel so far India's fight for freedom is recalled through a character or the horrors of the partition.

In *A Backward Place*,[34] Sudhir's friend, the old man Jaykar, is an old revolutionary who has spent an aggregate of fifteen years in various jails. In *A New Dominion*,[35] political confrontation is echoed in the arguments that Deepak the Joint Secretary has with Gerald his English counterpart at their Embassy. In independent India, Deepak is not willing to accept that India's relations with England go back over 200 years. To him they are nothing more than "the Dutch or French or any other ex-Colonial ex-power." The English, he argued, had foisted themselves "on us and it took all we had to throw you out again." (52) Indians had to learn to speak the other's language while they didn't "bother about ours." The association can be seen also in the graveyards where tombstones declared the dead Englishmen as having served in the army or civil services. There were graves of those whose wives and children had died in India of heat and sickness. There were also those who had been killed by native assassins. The home for the old had many English inmates who had spent their lives in India in positions of power and authority and treasured plaques that lauded their participation in the relief of Lucknow in the December of 1857.

In *Heat and Dust,*[14] Olivia's husband Douglas Rivers is the Assistant Collector at Satipur. As an English civil servant he "worked like a Trojan and never ceased to be calm and controlled" and was much esteemed by his colleagues and the Indians. But the English socialized only amongst themselves or with the princely Indians. One such Indian was the Nawab of Khatm, a neighbouring state. The Nawab came by his state in the way most such states came about. While he himself claimed that his ancestors had fought the Mahrattas, Rajputs, Mughals and British and when the last of them could not subdue him they offered him the lands and revenues of Khatm with the title of Nawab. The English version was that in the uprising at Satipur during the Mutiny, unlike the Raja of Satipur who had joined the Mutiny, the Nawab's ancestor had remained "loyal"—though often making sure which side to remain loyal to. He got his English title and the land revenues of Khatm. The present Nawab had a grand palace built in the 1820s and Major Minnies was his English political Agent.

The impact of the Mutiny had lingered in the British mind and they cherished their victory in prints of "Sir Henry Lawrence struck by a bullet in the Lucknow Residency" with which they decorated their homes. Olivia comes across many graves of those who died in the Mutiny. Douglas himself belonged to a family that had shaped the British empire in India. Rich Indians came to pay their respects to him on certain festivals and he hoped that when he had sons all of them would be in India. "Supposing things change—I mean what with Mr. Gandhi and these people." (93) Olivia interjects only to be reassured by Douglas that India needed them for a while longer. Ironically when Douglas has a son from his second wife Tessie, he could not return to India because there was nothing to return to, India having gained independence. Douglas has just reached retirement age and returned to England like most Englishmen.

If such was India's political history, India after independence is facing a welter of confusion. The old political ideologies are lost and a confused mixture of values survive the alien rule.

Radha in *To Whom She Will* had felt virtuous in the old days to be seen in "cotton saris and a husband who was often in prison." (12) But when she sees others enjoying the spoils of freedom, she sighs: "If he had lived today, he would have been a Minister." (24) But the author reminds us that he had been "too rigid, too literary, too quixotic . . . to ally himself with any party actually in power" (24) and would at best have remained an M.P. Radha casts away her cotton to wear bright, rich silk saris and heavy jewellery. If her husband had made the sacrifice of surrendering everything for India's freedom, her father Pandit Ram Bahadur Saxena who had also been a distinguished barrister gave up nothing. He retained his Englishness and lived in the same opulence after independence being much respected for it. It was no longer a matter of pride to travel in a third-class compartment and it took serious efforts on Radha's part to persuade her lodger, the intelligent Krishna Sen Gupta, to travel better. Status depended on power and what you could afford. This class-consciousness was derived from the British system in which such privileges symbolized superiority. What had united all Indians above class and caste was now dissolved into the very system they had fought against. It leaves idealists like Krishna Sen Gupta's parents disappointed, for "political reality had turned out to be rather different from the ideal." (257)

Lalaji in *The Nature of Passion* is able to bribe the new Deputy Minister when caught in a bribery and corruption case. His *rajasa* nature finds encouragement in the new political climate in India. His Son Chandra who is a civil servant cannot live within his salary; but having stepped into the chairs of his English counterpart, his wife Kanta and he must live like them, educating children in boarding schools, taking a holiday in the hills all of which must be paid for by Lalaji.

In *Esmond in India*, Har Dayal is like Pandit Ram Bahadur Saxena of Jhabvala's earlier novel. A friend of Ram Nath, Har Dayal had not been a Congress worker giving up his money or position or earning a police record. When the English had the power he "looked just like English gentlemen" and after independence he had taken care to have friends who "all looked like Indian Congressmen." In post-independent India, Har Dayal was well-placed, serving on many committees and living as comfortably as his father did. Ram Nath, the political idealist, was left ignored in a ramshackle building. It is this that irks Lakshmi who had, like Radha of the earlier novel, taken pride in bearing her husband's sacrifices. Their son Narayan, a brilliant doctor serving the tribals in the interiors, is considered a no-good match for Har Dayal's daughter Shakuntala because he does not make as much money as a city-doctor. Lakshmi, disillusioned, asks Ram Nath not to stand in Narayan's way with "words of duty and sacrifice" in the changed values of a politically free India. In *The Householder,* the young college lecturer Prem is one of those victims of the English education-system wanting only a white-collar job. The wages are meagre and he is unable to meet his responsibilities of being a householder but there is nothing better he can do. The prestige of being a "Professor" is never far from his consciousness.

Sarla Devi in *Get Ready for Battle* is rejected by her husband for her political idealism. He believes in those symbols of power and authority that the English introduced. He even adopts a western manner of living. His wife on the other hand is engaged in fighting for the rights of the slum-dwellers of Bundi Busti against all government and social agencies and moneyed people like her husband Gulzarilal and son Vishnu who are engaged in increasing their power-base or money.

A Backward Place is India in which no encouragement is given to the intelligent, the enterprising. The needy Jaykar the old revolutionary does his best to highlight failures in his paper *Second Thoughts* but is reconciled to sharing his son's government accommodation. He coaxes Sudhir on the other hand to give up "this effete little empire of clerks and civil servants" to go out into the fields to build "a new India from the foundation upwards." But it was not easy to do so unless everyone worked together as in Jaykar's day when their only aim had been to throw the English out. In the present-day, there were so many things to work for but no one knew where to begin. The ilk of Mrs. Kaul had large ambitions "but their conceptions—based as they were not so much on any profound inner need as a something heard or read about and found desirable were so vague and weak that everything that came of them also tended to be vague and weak." (209)

In *A New Dominion,* Jhabvala goes over to those of the English who chose to remain in India after Independence and were treated with suspicion or neglect. In the new country, the charitable works of the missionary Miss Charlotte, who had been in India a long, long time, were being questioned. In parliament "questions were often asked . . . about proselytising missionaries and Christian missions of varying denominations were being closed all over the country." (12) Rao Sahib an erstwhile prince-turned-politician explains that Miss Charlotte's philanthropic work cannot be allowed by the Government of India because "the giant task ahead of us is one that must be solved not through the individual efforts of foreigners whose presence in our midst is an anachronism but through our own machinery of parliamentary democracy and nationalised socialism." (72) The new nation is proud of forging ahead in the production of small ancillaries while other social-welfare works are neither allotted to rich industrialists nor encouraged to be done by private parties. The politicians hold immense power in the new set-up and they generally foist their fads and foibles and verbosity on the unsuspecting masses while lining their own pockets.

In *Heat and Dust,* if Olivia's story provided political history, the young narrator's story by contrast provides the post-independent dilemma. The narrator is first warned to look after her possessions carefully lest they be stolen. The young English boy Chidananda whom she meets later had been robbed of all his belongings when he had come to renunciate all to find the path to peace. The narrator is then warned about the food; her "hippie" friend who dares to eat what he gets when begging for his food comes down with a severe attack of dysentery. What had been the Collector's house at Satipur now housed three different offices. The Nawab's palace at Khatm is in utter disrepair but his descendants who cannot live in the present-day India and are in England were "still negotiating with the Government of India for a sale but so far over all these years no price had been agreed upon. There are no other bidders." The buses were packed to bursting point. The hospital that Dr. Saunders took special pride in was overflowing with in-patients and out-patients that Dr. Gopal found impossible to cope with. The ambulance needed repair, no additions were made to the hospital which was indeed short of staff, equipment and space.

A slightly different kind of political encounter occurs in *Three Continents*.[37] The Rawul is waiting to hoist the stars and stripes as well as his flag of the Fourth World. Even though Lindsay, the mother of Michael and Harriet and from whose family "Propinquity" has come down to them, has no positive objections, the idea is strongly vetoed by Barbara, their father's current girlfriend. Although she has nothing to gain or lose, she still holds her head on her shoulders and can see naught that could have given the Rawul this privilege and that on the fourth of July. Of course the Rawul's princedom and privileges too are a thing of the past, something Harriet and Michael are to discover much later in their lives. But the dupe is carried through the major portion of their lives together. This novel is dated in contemporaneity so that it allows for little more than this on this front.

IV

From an examination of their novels, it can safely be concluded that political confrontation between India and Britain is an essential ingredient in Markandaya's and Jhabvala's stories. That Britain, without having fought any wars with armies of its own men, should have so insidiously worked itself into a paramount power governing India, rankled in the hearts of the Indians. What actually aggravated the resentment in the Indians was the British aloofness and their presumed superiority. At first the orderliness of British rule had brought appreciation, respect, even confidence and affection from the Indians, but that gradually changed to suspicion, disappointment and anger and an indiscriminate criticism of everything English. No patriotic Indian could ignore these developments, less so an artist and writer. To defy Britain, to oust them from a land that rightfully belonged to the Indians became the cause. The heroic thing was to work for that cause. Markandaya's heroes or heroines, for it has been said of her that like Shakespeare she has only heroines and no heroes, are pitted against forces that weaken the cause. Political confrontation is the centre of action not as historical documentation but in the artistic way of providing a background for the protagonists's struggle, by creating the environment for all action, so that actions and reactions are ranged against it. In this way the stories are provided a plot and the characters become psychological studies. Their action against the despoiling effects of foreign rule in every form provide the drama. Markandaya's expatriate status and her being married to an Englishman enable her to see differences in the role of the Britons in their own country and homes. There they are urbane, humane and civilized but the role of the English as rulers in India was marred by their being ruthless, overbearing, supercilious and imperious. The core of the conflict is centred in the latter role. But Markandaya is objective in her analysis of such a confrontation. India had been in the forefront of civilization but had allowed itself to be split into small entities instead of being united as a force. Indians were therefore beaten into submission and hunched up where they could have stood upright. The freedom movement had proved that India could again be whole. As the Dewan's daughter Usha in *The Golden Honeycomb* says, "it was an experiment, to see if discipline would hold, whatever . . . discipline did hold. It was like a revelation. We didn't believe you know, never really believed how much force there could be, if you trust yourself . . . so powerful. All of us. All the fright gone. They couldn't have touched us whatever they did." (398-99) The didacticism contained in this idea by implication makes her writing a literature of concern. Committed to the beliefs that wrongs must be righted, her novels confirm that zeal. Her political belief is that India and Britain can only live in amity if they respect each other's sovereignty and effect a reconciliation in the spirit of forgive and forget. Even individual personal relations are not easy if misgivings of such a political nature linger. There is, one may add, no finality in her novels; no victory or loss, because reconciliation is compromise, not outright victory or defeat.

Ruth Prawer Jhabvala also brings to bear upon her novels her own expatriate position in India. Born in one country, brought up in another and living in a third, her cosmopolitanism provides her a striking objectivity. It is understandable that she does not delve into political history as incisively as Markandaya, nevertheless she uses it as a silhouette against which to trace her characters. The two groups of princes and freedom-fighters were particularly shaped by this political history. The princes who were in many ways the lackeys of the ruling nation are plummetted out of their privileged positions in independent India and it remained in each of them individually to retain his hold on the ruling class, by entering business or politics. Those who didn't are a pitiable lot. The freedom-fighters on the other hand who had made many sacrifices and had undergone many hardships were ignored by the new government. It was for the shrewd, the turncoat to make his individual gains. The idealism that brought independence was gone. Ironically the same opportunism and money power, which had brought the English into power and were fought against to restore freedom to India, were the tools of the new powers that came into being. Jhabvala's mode is ironic vision, so that she introduces fun while exposing the hypocrisies of the new wine in an old bottle. The bureaucratic system that was introduced by the English to operate by way of written orders and legal principles went haywire because the bureaucracy became unwieldy. Offices and officers proliferated. As Pearl S. Buck says, having been a subject-race for so long, Indians got used to being cared for by the ruler. With the British gone this role fell to the Government which was held responsible for feeding and clothing and governing them. Colonialism had produced the muddle so that "there was rot at the top . . . in the thousands of young intellectuals trained in English schools for jobs that did not exist except in the limited civil service."[37] There was a general lackadaisical attitude towards all work which Jhabvala satirizes in her novels. The earlier novels echo political confrontation as a social irony but the later novels end on a note of interrogation. They are corrective in approach and have as much a didactic value as Markandaya's novels. But the tone is not didactic and therein lies their artistic quality.

NOTES

1. S.C. Roy Choudhary, *Social, Cultural and Economic History of India* (New Delhi, 1980), p. 3.
2. *Indian English Prose*, ed. D. Ramakrishna (Delhi, 1980), p. 161.
3. S.C. Roy Choudhary, *History of Modern India* (Delhi, 1980), p. 133.
4. V.P. Menon, *The Story of the Integration of the Indian States* (Orient Longman, 1961), p. 5.
5. *Ibid.*, pp. 6-7.
6. *Ibid.*, p. 7.
7. Percival Spear, *A History of India* (Great Britain, 1970), 2, p. 121.
8. *Ibid.*, p. 118.
9. S.C. Roy Choudhary, *Social, Cultural and Economic History of India*, p. 8.
10. Percival Spear, 2, p. 123.
11. *Writers in East-West Encounter: New Cultural Bearings*, ed. Guy Amirthanayagam (Hong-Kong, 1982), pp. 68-70.
12. G.M. Trevelyan, *History of England* (O.M. Longman), p. 551.
13. R.C. Agarwal, *Constitutional History of India and National Movement* (New Delhi, 1981), p. 35.
14. G.M. Trevelyan, p. 675.
15. Percival Spear, 2, p. 176.
16. V.B. Kulkarni, *British Statesmen in India* (Orient Longman, 1961), p. 353.
17. *Ibid.*, p. 359.

18. *Ibid.*, p. 362.
19. Kamala Markandaya, *Some Inner Fury* (London, 1955).
20. Kamala Markandaya, "On Images," paper presented at the seminar on Socio-Literature (East-West Centre for Cultural Interchange, Honolulu, August 1973).
21. Kamala Markandaya, *A Silence of Desire* (London, 1960).
22. Margaret P. Joseph, *Kamala Markandaya* (New Delhi, 1980), p. 49.
23. Kamala Markandaya, *A Handful of Rice* (Delhi, 1966).
24. Kamala Markandaya, *The Nowhere Man* (London, 1973).
25. Kamala Markandaya, *Two Virgins* (New Delhi, 1977).
26. Kamala Markandaya, *The Golden Honeycomb* (New York, 1978).
27. Kamala Markandaya, *Nectar in a Sieve* (Bombay, 1955).
28. K.R. Srinivas Iyengar, p. 446.
29. Kamala Markandaya, *The Coffer Dams* (Delhi: Hind, 1969).
30. Ruth Prawer Jhabvala, *To Whom She Will* (London, 1955).
31. Ruth Prawer Jhabvala, *The Nature of Passion* (London, 1956).
32. Ruth Prawer Jhabvala, *Esmond in India* (London, 1958).
33. Ruth Prawer Jhabvala, *Get Ready for Battle* (Suffolk, 1983).
34. Ruth Prawer Jhabvala, *A Backward Place* (Delhi, 1965).
35. Ruth Prawer Jhabvala, *A New Dominion* (London, 1972).
36. Ruth Prawer Jhabvala, *Heat and Dust* (Delhi, 1975).
37. Ruth Prawer Jhabvala, *Three Continents* (London: John Murray, 1987).
38. See Pearl S. Buck, *My Several Worlds* (Methuen, 1955).

The Religio-Philosophical Encounter

The whole philosophy of life and existence of the East and the West is different. To the West "individuality is . . . the peak and purpose of the whole cosmic process."[1] The western men think of egos and set themselves against the play of nature "with an egocentric tenacity."[2] The occidental man presses onward in the historic human battle to dominate the earth and its elements; to control the vegetable, animal, mineral and even sub-atomic kingdoms. He believes himself to be the most consequential member of creation who must prevail over the others. His "fervent faith in the perfectibility of human affairs" lays emphasis on "better planning, technology, a wider spread of education and the opening of opportunities for all."[3] Western philosophy is rational, pragmatic, scientific and consequently materialistic; Western materialism being derived from the Greeks who placed more emphasis on reason. The East thinks not of individual lives but of life, in which the individual is "merely a part of the phenomenon." He feels closer to outer objects and is intimately related to them. Swami Vivekananda explains that the Hindus believed that every living creature is an emanation of the same pure white light of the Divine Being.[4] The centre is located in the body but the "circumference is now-here" and this centre changes from body to body so that "death is but change." There are innumerable manifestations of this "spark of the Divine" as it passes from one personality to the other till it reaches perfection after which there is no change. In this context therefore Man is seen to be striving to release the soul from the pangs of rebirth in which the East believes lies "the final flowing of the success of the successful man."[5] When human beings realize that they are really instruments for the expression of spirit, they outgrow individualism and espouse the cause of fellowmen because they are expressions of the same spirit. In this way they break down the egoistic claim that life and universe is centred around man. Universality of individuality entails universal love for each and every creature and espouses "ahimsa" or non-violence. Philosophies also give shape to religion and although no man is born to any religion, religious differences are aggravated when "a moral assertion is used to express an attitude of the man making the assertion . . . to show forth or evince his attitude. The attitude is concerned with the action which he asserts to be good."[6] One of the chief distinctions between the Hindu and Christian religions is this: the Christian religion teaches that "each human soul had its beginnings at its birth into this world . . . whereas the Hindu religion asserts that the spirit of man is an emanation of the Eternal Being and had no more a beginning."[7] Another difference is that the Hindus worship God in his numerous forms, which appears to the Christian a contradiction of the age-long Indian Philosophy of *Advaita*. C. Rajagopalachari explains this practice by stating that "god is sought in a medley of forms for God is a supreme Medley."[8] The different shapes and sizes impress on Hindus God's formlessness and incomprehensibility. How best can his transcendent quality as well as all-pervasiveness be realized unless He is given a hundred different forms? Almost every religion believes in the worship of God-form or symbols, names and God-men. Each of these forms is something positive, concrete and shows a passionate devotion to God in each of these forms. There should be no question of war between the varying idols, symbols being a tacit and wise acceptance of all the forms. Symbols and rites are equally holy for each worshipper concerned. But when the British political power was firmly established in India, the Evangelicals viewed India as a breeding ground of idolatry in which they believed millions of souls were "rushing to perdition without a chance of Christian salvation."[9] The Radicals, with their faith in reason as strong as the Evangelical's confidence in the Gospel, joined hands with them to denounce the religious practices of India and bring the Christian West to the East. It was their bigotry which was bad and which condoned its own superstitions and found fault with the other's. Christopher Isherwood, in the Introduction to *Teachings of Swami Vivekananda*, mentions that the Archbishop of Canterbury refused to attend Parliament of Religions in Chicago because it implied the equality of all religions. And a Catholic priest felt that there could be some truths in "heathenism" but that did not imply that all religions were equally good. Both are striking examples of Christian bigotry. The Holy Man is also important to all religions. Hinduism believes that "the soul can receive impulses from another soul and from nothing else."[10] The development of the spiritual side of man is not necessarily to be proportionate to a high order of intellectual development. He is deemed to have fulfilled the duties and obligations of that stage of life to which he is born and ready to abandon all worldly pursuits when he turns to seek Eternal Love. He makes complete renunciation seeking persistently spiritual knowledge and striving to excel in love and compassion. It is years of meditation, discipline and inquiry that make him a Guru. He is above religion and his duty is with the poor. Dr. Radhakrishnan clarifies that "Nature is not opposed to spirit. It is attachment to nature that is inconsistent with spiritual dignity. Asceticism is opposed not to enjoyment but to attachment."[11] In Christianity the parish priest guides his parish in many ways. He renders service to humanity, in a bid to ultimately inherit "the Kingdom of God."

Finally, the East believes that Man in his earthly life is a victim of Time. He cannot work the changes. There are periods when everything supports the hero-conqueror and he rides the wave. At such a time even his faults and deficiencies turn to his advantage. "Time proceeds in cycles, now expanding, now contracting.... No one can battle time. Its tides are mysterious. One must learn to accept them and submit to their unalterable rhythm."[12] The relentless flow of time swallows individuals, places them at the mercy of the destructive forces of death—diseases, plagues, warfare, human tyranny and injustice. Time can wipe out the blooms of realms and towns and crumble even the ruins to dust. Fatalism and stoic suffering consequently become an accepted creed. The East destroys evil by suffering till the evil is nothing and becomes instead positive enjoyment. The West minimizes evil by conquering it. Idealism, mysticism and fatalism of the East are ranged against the pragmatism, materialism and individualism of the West.

Swami Vivekananda asked, "Who knows which is the true ideal? The apparent power and strength as held in the West or the fortitude in suffering of the East?" When history brought the two races together, the two divergent philosophies came into conflict because of latent differences. Attempts to bridge that gap were made with the first Indian writers in English. Raja Ram Mohan Roy realized with sorrow that "the bigoted Christian was as conceited as the bigoted Hindu."[13] In 1821, he made a bold and sustained onslaught on the forces of prejudice and reaction in his weekly paper, *Sambad Kaumudi*. Keshab Chunder Sen tried to forge links between Christianity and Hinduism which he felt were not really incompatible with each other. Sri Aurobindo's prose symphony *Life Divine* lies like "a metaphysical bridge between the West and East."[14] He was never blind to the eastern spiritual reality behind all that western material facade. Mahatma Gandhi's ethics too were rooted in Indian tradition with close affiliation with Christian tradition. Even Nehru, "a prophet of modernity," remarked in his Azad Memorial Lecture: "I have often wondered that if our race forgot the Buddha, the Upanishads and the great epics, what then will it be like."[15] In more recent writing, there have been philosophical novels like Dilip Kumar Roy's *The Upward Spiral* and Raja Rao's *The Serpent and the Rope* and *The Cat and Shakespeare*.

Kamala Markandaya and Ruth Prawer Jhabvala in their total conception of the gamut of East-West relations touch upon religious philosophical encounters because they are impediments in the path of a fruitful linking of hands. In Markandaya there is a direct confrontation as each side is steeped in its convictions. All the major issues of philosophy and religion crop up in her novels. In Jhabvala such direct confrontation crops up only in the later novels. In the earlier novels there is an ironic approach, Western in character and chiefly ephemeral. The chief issues in their novels can be classified accordingly: (a) Kindred Souls (b) Time and Ready Acceptance (c) Conflict of Symbols and Superstitions and (d)

Conflict of Holy Men.

II

Kamala Markandaya's characters, Indian and English, embody their own respective philosophies and religious beliefs to the point of being incomprehensible to the other. In this stark pessimism, there are stray rays of hope when a character on either side makes an effort at understanding the other's religious and philosophical leanings.

To take the aspect of "Kindred Souls." In all Markandaya's novels, the Indian characters strongly uphold the tradition of universal life and love, in their concern for animals, in vegetarianism, in providing shelter to destitute and deformed relatives and attitudes to death. Belief in universal individualism enjoins active charity, meekness and humaneness. In all conflict with evil, the method to be used is love and not force, for in using evil methods to defeat evil, it is evil that wins. In a letter written to Margaret P. Joseph, Markandaya admits: "I detest cruelty to any living being."[16] This attitude seems innate in her Hindu psyche and finds its manifestations in loving descriptions of animals, the virtues of vegetarianism and respect for all life.

In *Nectar in a Sieve,* the heroine Rukmani, on her way to her new home in her husband Nathan's cart, is glad to see the bullocks unyoked and led to "the small pool of water near which we had stopped, giving them each a handful of hay. After that rest the beasts "began stepping, jauntily again." (3) The coming of the tannery to the village brings an upheaval in the fortunes of Rukmani and Nathan. Carted away to the city in search of a son, Rukmani even in her tribulation is concerned over the bullocks's sores: '"The animal is not well,' I say to the man. He shrugs: 'what can I do? I have no other. I must make these trips since they are my livelihood'." (140) The cartman is forced to compromise his instincts of kindness for the sake of physical survival. Rukmani, despite her upheavals, is a woman of fortitude. She retains her instinctive love and kindness to adopt the leper Puli, with whom she returns to her village after Nathan dies and whom she entrusts to Dr. Kenny's care.

In *Possession,* Valmiki, growing up to become a famous painter in England under Caroline's patronage, could not shake off his belief that "a part of God dwelt in every man and would one day reunite with the divine whole." (154) It lies at the root of his strict vegetarianism even in alienation. "Killing has no appeal for me," he says and Anasuya notices that despite his utterance there is "no trace of the repugnance that would have been the old crude reaction to what was in deep conflict not only with his inheritance of compassion but with the very nature of his religion." (178) British contact had blunted his prejudices but not his belief that "Animals aren't created for men." He takes the death of his pet monkey Minou as punishment for the "violation of this precept." Anasuya, the Indian writer, holds a similar belief but she warns him that a lot of people do subscribe to the view that they are like "the whole of Christendom." Valmiki firmly believed that "Animals are created in their own right" and therefore felt that he must have stopped believing this when he bought the monkey, of which he "took possession like a god, for ends of my own." Such compassion extends to his love for Ellie, the Jewish girl, ugly and scarred by the war and sick with its horrors. He loses part of his spiritualism when he resorts to painting her in the nude to focus on her beauty. Yet when those paintings are lauded, he considers it blasphemy to exalt man-made over man. Caroline by contrast is materialistic. She has paid for Valmiki, brought him to England, pored care and money into nurturing his talent for her own ends. She endures Ellie as a help and suffers no compunctions in slapping the girl for breaking her best china. To Caroline, India's apparent non-violence and universal love is hypocrisy. "India's full of cruelty," she says. When Anasuya says it is different, Caroline sniggers, "Different. Of course it is. It's Christians behaving like methodical beasts. Not Hindus doing the same thing haphazard." (77) Anasuya being Indian sees that behind Caroline's calm veneer is her sense of secret shame for having hurt Ellie. Even the good house-keeper Mrs. Peabody says about Ellie: "she gives you the creeps." But

Valmiki's relations with Ellie become more intimate and he even gets her pregnant. Woman is the centre of Hindu society; Indian philosophy and religion enjoin "a great respect for motherhood through the sanctification and inviolability of marriage."[17] Valmiki felt remorse at this positive interdict but Anasuya adds that an "atavistic reaction against unsanctioned defloration was common even in relaxed societies." (201) Ellie commits suicide; Val is saddened but knows that death is only change. He strikes a new liaison with Annabel. Caroline enlightens her on the circumstances of Ellie's death and Annabel castigates Val for having got her into trouble and getting out quick, "before the whiff of suicide could offend your nostrils and curl up those holy eastern sentiments of yours about the sanctity of life." (201)

In *A Handful of Rice,* Ravi the vagabond hero finds shelter from the police in Apu the tailor's house. Despite his bad habits, Ravi is still in his "primal" state as far as philosophies are concerned. His love and compassion is reflected in his actions. He throws the plantain leaf on which his *idlies* were served to the cows nosing in the gutters. Apu's wife Jayamma too "had been brought up to respect every living being as the fragmentation of an eternal God." (55) When Ravi becomes rebellious and materialistic he loses his latent concern and love for living creatures. In a dejected mood he kicked the stones in his path and when a dog prowled past sniffing the gutter he picked up a jagged stone to throw at it but was held back by an urge, older and stronger. Apu had exemplified his universal love in supporting needy relatives and the cripple Kumaran even on his meagre resources. After Apu's death, Ravi turns out Thangam and her none-too-good husband, the cripple Kumaran, and even commits incest with his mother-in-law. The reversal in his nature, his descent into gross crudities is because of his scant respect for life and love. They are seen as part of his city influences deemed western-oriented and materialistic. No love can grow here so that Ravi's untainted love for Nalini grows sour. Ravi is not totally converted to western pragmatism and still believes he will be reborn but he does not want to be reborn in his present state.

In *The Coffer Dams,* the English technologists and Indian

engineers close their ranks after the accident at the dam site when the lives of Indians and a few English are lost. When two Indian bodies cannot be traced, the other labourers strike work. Rawlings, the quick-tempered Englishman, cannot understand why the fuss is made. But Clinton's wife, Helen, has tried getting under the skins of the Indians and reasons with her husband: "they believe the spirit will not be freed, until its body has been reverenced." (177) Clinton cannot understand such beliefs. Neither can Rawlings understand what Krishnan means by saying they will suffer "spiritual torments," if the body is deemed nothing when the spirit is gone. The body indeed is nothing, "it is the spirit that matters," (179) Krishnan asserts, but it is a matter of equal respect for their beliefs as the English wanted for their own. The English duly reverenced the body laying it in state till Doomsday and resurrection. To this end the English made sure the loam was freshly turned so that the dead could lie easy. The Indians preferring "not to lie and moulder" punctiliously observed funeral rites, burning the dead body and sending the ashes—as the English contemptuously thought—bowling merrily along on the river.

Helen has imbibed the spirit of understanding and love for kindred souls. She confesses to the tribal technician Bashiam: "Our animals—we could learn from them, but we're Christians you know, arrogant people, so we deprive them of their rights. Deny them. Pretend they haven't got any. . . . We don't allow them to (move) in case they yield us one ounce less of their flesh. Where is our instinct for pity? Blunted. We've cut ourselves off from our heritage. We've forgotten what we knew." (138) Helen has compassion and love and when wandering in the forest she would embrace stray dogs, rub flea-powder into their yellow coats. At night she fondly observed the deer that came near her bungalow every night "despite the dam, the clutter of machinery, the flood lights," that were all symbols of man's achievements.

Gopal Rao could not get over his non-violence. Vegetarianism was part of his upbringing. He tried hard "not to think about these beefy men, the master builders who could stomach anything, flesh and blood and kidneys that reeked as he knew from watching them feed." (171) He squirmed when he saw real flesh and blood at the accident site much to the chagrin of his friend Lefevre who like the other Englishmen wondered why a dead body should be so repulsive to his friend for whom only the soul mattered.

In *The Nowhere Man,* Srinivas and his wife Vasantha, domiciled in England for a long time, are still strictly vegetarian. After Vasantha's death, Srinivas invites Mrs. Pickering to share his home but does not yield to her non-vegetarianism. His companionship with Mrs. Pickering is based on compassion. The turbulence and violence that follows the wake of racist agitation in England is repulsive to him. It is alien to his spiritual make-up and he cannot endure it. When Vasantha dies of tuberculosis in England he cremates her in the electric crematorium but according to his religious beliefs he takes a casket of her ashes to immerse in the river. While spilling it in the Thames, he is chided by the English policeman for polluting the river but he pathetically explains that it was only his wife. His association with Mrs. Pickering brings in him an understanding of the Christian religion and he helps her to decorate a tree on Christmas to place by a window for the neighbours to see. He had been quite aloof before, so the new gesture was well-approved by his neighbours who believed that at last he had become civilized.

In *Two Virgins*, Saroja and Lalitha grow up in the Hindu tradition and imbibe a respect for all living beings. They believe that "you couldn't destroy soul" though Lalitha was told by her Christian teacher Miss Mendoza that "souls did not enter other bodies. They went straight up to heaven or down into hell or were cooped up in purgatory which was an in-between place for doing penance in" (6) till the day of resurrection when a bugle call awoke the dead. The animals had been created for man and God had given man dominion over the beasts. But Lalitha was not convinced. Saroja feels concerned when Manikkam wants to sell a barren cow to the butcher. She feels relieved that his wife being "a good Hindu" would never consent to cow-slaughter. Saroja watched as Mannikam's wife carefully bathed the cow's udders and rubbed coconut fat into the splits. She was often heard to say, "should I grudge her a mouthful of grass after all the milk that has flowed from her these past years?" (6) Appa too was of the opinion that animals should never be grudged what men did not want. He had planted prickly pear on his boundary which the donkey with "white circles round its eyes like eye-shadow and velvety lips" with a tongue and palate tough enough tackled. Saroja's love flows unrestrained for all animals and she feels pity for the patient little ponies at the Smithy's whose weary looks and the smell of their charred hoof made her distraught. These animals sometimes died in the shafts and drivers whose livelihood depended on them sometimes whipped them but passersby would get angry and restrain them. Hindu philosophy enjoined that when men used animals, they were not to encroach its integrity and be circumspect. Markandaya makes this novel a spirited defence of her own Hindu beliefs and little else so that structurally the novel suffers—none of these defences or invectives and diatribes against Christianity have any particular purpose. Amma is heard to say that Muslims and Europeans being flesh-eaters are callous of animals's feelings. But the author soon corrects such a direct accusation with Lalitha declaring that Miss Mendoza had taught them that despite being flesh-eaters Europeans were kind to animals, and with a later remark by Appa that "Muslims, Europeans and Hindus could be equally callous about animals."

According to Hindu philosophy the soul finds release only after its present embodiment of flesh and bones is fully destroyed on death. Appa's compatriot Rangu was cremated when he died in police action and his ashes were immersed in the river which absorbs both joys and sorrows because it is eternal, ever-flowing. In *The Golden Honeycomb* once again, the destruction of life is averred by Indians. Indian villagers shake their fists at the two Europeans who have killed the birds. One of the reasons why the Dewan keeps his distance from the British Resident is that the latter ate "animal carcasses." The Western philosophy of reverencing the body till the soul can once more claim it at resurrection is referred to in the syce who takes care to note where the dead horse lay.

Through all these stories Markandaya projects the issue of "kindred souls" out of her tenacious need to cling to her heritage in alienation. Except in *A Handful of Rice* where it is used to delineate Ravi's character and his later degradation, in the other novels there is a conscious mention to introduce tension in the plot and more chiefly to educate the unknowing readers.

Fatalism is a creed among Indians. Man is buffetted by the tides of time. Such Indian stoicism is always questioned by western pragmatism. In *Nectar in a Sieve,* Rukmani is reconciled to the vagaries of her life. Like a patient Job she tides her crises and patiently waits for times to be better. Her forbearance in adversity, her passive acceptance of things, irks her "benefactor." Dr. Kenny cannot understand such passivity. "Times are better, times are better. Times will not be better for many months. Meanwhile you will suffer and die, you meek suffering fools. Why do you keep this ghastly silence," (43-44) he shouts at her. He believed that man must fight the odds for his survival because these are symptoms of his heroic qualities. Like Melville's Ahab, man must fight, demand, "cry out for help—do something." Rukmani is aghast at such violence. She admits helplessness before His will. She questions, "What can we do?" Kenny advises her to "cry out if you want. It is no use whatsoever to suffer in silence. Who will succour the drowning man if he does not clamour for his life." (113) He sees "no grandeur in want or in endurance." (113)

Rukmani's philosophy is one of fortitude. She believes that "a man's spirit" is "given to him to rise above his misfortunes." Man's wants are many and cannot always be fulfilled. "Want is our companion from birth to death, familiar as the seasons of the earth, varying only in degree. What profit to bewail that which has always been and cannot change." (114) It is only such fortitude that sustains Old Granny who has lived alone making a meagre living by selling vegetables. "It is not unbearable. One gets used to it," she says. Kenny remains unconvinced. "Do you think," he asks Rukmani, "spiritual grace comes from being in want or from suffering?" Rukmani has been taught to bear her sorrows in silence. She sees them as a chastening process. Kenny despairs of India and its people if they must be so fatalistic. His western rationalism advocates a certain amount of planning, thinking about the future, chalking out a plan of action. Total surrender to time is amazing. Rukmani cannot plan, "How can we? It is not within our means. . . . We are in God's hands." (131) The agrarian people are dependent on weather for their livelihood: "The calamities of the land belong to it alone, born of wind and rain and weather, immensities not to be tempered by man or his creations. To those who live by the land there must always come a time of hardship, of fear and of hunger, even as there are years of plenty. This is one of the truths of our existence, as those who live by the land know." (174) Rukmani thereby explains the need for stoicism. There is no pessimism in this but a deep-rooted faith in God's mercies. When Kali's hut is destroyed in the storm she is thankful that at least "it stood until the worst was over." Rukmani too is of the same faith. When her barren daughter Ira is forsaken by her husband, she consoles her saying "we are all in God's hands and He is merciful. These are the vicissitudes of life just as a good harvest follows a drought to give us another chance of belief in His mercy. Nothing is unbearable and man's indomitable spirit can help him surmount those tribulations by endurance." Ironically, the village huts are uprooted in the storm, while the tannery withstands the onslaught suggesting that western rationality has the timber to survive, to fight destiny. However, the westerner Kenny with all his rationality could not save his marriage from breaking down.

Some Inner Fury again shows man as insignificant in the cosmic scheme. Govind, after his college studies, is involved in the activities of the freedom struggle. He is also secretly in love with his foster-brother Kit's wife, Premala. The "very fates seemed aware" of his problem and tried to help him. His well-meaning parents advise him to stay on but "the fates once flouted grew thereafter malicious . . . they flung their trammels wide and caught us all and drew us in together until none of us could break away, not one. There was no escape from those triple-meshed nets." (77) It was the last evening that the family was together, before Govind's activities and Premala's unhappiness produce the catastrophe. On reflection Mira discovers there had been signals of their foreboding sadness but they "saw no shadow, heard no whisper, to warn us it was the last time." But she also knows that they could have done nothing about it. "We should still have gone our way, moving in orbits we ourselves created and could not help creating because we were what we were." (83-84) Mira is aware that character is destiny. Of his own free will, Govind has determined his character.

In *A Silence of Desire,* Dandekar exerts rationalism against Sarojini's blind faith. But even he is ready to give up because "the practical difficulties were too great and apart from that in prudence one did not pit one's wits against fate, if it seemed set against action. God's will be done." (115) Val's mother in *Possession* is like Rukmani in *Nectar in a Sieve*. She does not complain of dying at forty: "Hers was a generation thoroughly conditioned and ground into acceptance." Ravi the hero of *A Handful of Rice* rejects the "excessive endurance" that had only brought him acute poverty in the village. He was sickened by the thought that "things would never be any better, knew they were lucky to stand still, for the only other way was downward. It was this knowing the worst, the hopelessness of it plus the way people accepted their lot and even thanked God it was no worse." (49) He wanted to flee this "culture for the breeding of suffering" and he hopes to escape it when he goes to the city. But he finds that the tailor Apu into whose house he had sought shelter, is as addled as his own father had been, that their state was unalterable. Ravi is like Iqbal in Khushwant Singh's *A Train to Pakistan* in censuring India for dispensing with proof and relying merely on faith. Ravi wished to shape his future but Apu's Jayamma believes it sacrilegious to anticipate happy events. The future was Heaven's prerogative and if provoked it could blight happiness. Nothing guaranteed happiness; it was fleet of foot so who could hold happiness, the crippled Kumaran tells Ravi's wife Nalini. Ravi did not want to put so much trust in God, "such things were for those of another generation." But his wife Nalini submits her future to God's care and delivers her dying father Apu into His hands. Ravi feels a sense of loss in surrendering his old convictions and actually seeks only a momentary escape in his defiance.

The Coffer Dams repeats the theme of acceptance. The tribals of the forests near Malnad are used to the vagaries of life. When they were asked to vacate their land for the camp for British technologists, they just got up and went. They were used to seeing the river as only "a trickle that did not percolate through to the shallowest irrigation channels of their parched fields" (9) when the rains failed. And at other times, in heavy rain, they saw it inundate their lands, drown their huts and crops, "At both times they prayed to God, they never blamed Him. It was their fate." (9) The English team contrarily makes a rigid schedule in which they must complete their work because "a man's proper concern" is "this reaching for a star and the grasping of it in fulfilment of oaths made to himself." (19) A considerable tension generates in which many lives are lost but the dam is completed before the first rains. This is the first story where western pragmatism is seen to triumph which may be a considerable influence of Markandaya's stay abroad. The conflict of the disparate philosophies becomes necessary to generate conflict and is therefore not superfluous. In *The Nowhere Man,* when Vasantha receives the shocking news of her son's death she is visibly upset momentarily and must be shielded away from the public eye by an English neighbour. But she "had elements in her that would keep her upright, not only now but later, when the blows were not imaginary and crowded them or so it seemed. It was just that it took some time and some calling upon inner resources." (31-32) Her alien-bred sons could only clap their emotions instantly with available disguises.

In *Two Virgins,* Aunt Alamelu and Amma are votaries of acceptance of fate. Aunt Alamelu believes that it was fate that took her husband early in life in an epidemic and "how can you guard that?" Amma shares Aunt Alamelu's beliefs and Nalini, the sick girl, had it written on "her forehead from the day she was born" that she would die so early. Such death was tragic but "God is good and one must have faith in his boundless wisdom." (75)

In *The Golden Honeycomb,* Bawajiraj II's wife Shanta is resigned to her secondary role as his wife. In her novels Markandaya uses this philosophical aspect chiefly to delineate her characters.

She makes her Indians stoical but not pessimistic. Fortitude makes them strong in themselves and their actions do not suggest that they suffer because of its weakness. It is a way of thought which is not necessarily inferior to western rationalism and pragmatism. It makes her characters stand out in themselves. Even in *Two Virgins*--her weakest novel—Aunt Alamelu and Amma are seen as traditional but strong Indian women able to support their convictions.

Religion is realizing God. Dr. Radhakrishnan has explained that the supreme reality is difficult to grasp and impossible to define.[11] The inadequacy of our concept is reconciled to a negation of all that God is not. So that religion is the experience of reality and should have nothing to do with the religious doctrine because it is concerned with the religious feeling. The finite mind believes that the highest reality appears to possess a number of perfections. The conception of a personal God is the fusion of the highest logical truth with the deepest religious conviction. God is an object of genuine worship and reverence, not a non-ethical deity indifferent to man's needs and fears. But Man, in following his own strict set of practices to appease that God, self-righteously negates all other beliefs and practices. His own practices he deems religious, those of the other superstitious.

Rukmani in *Nectar in a Sieve* is desperate for a son which is considered a blessing of God. She visits her village temple and with her mother "would pray and pray before the deity, imploring for help until we were giddy." She prays with the knowledge that "Gods have other things to do: they cannot attend to the pleas of every suppliant who dares to raise his cares to heaven." (18) With Dr. Kenny's medical care she bears another child—a son and then five more—and she accepts them as God's blessings. When the rains fail, Rukmani, like the other villagers, takes it as God's punishment to them. She took a pumpkin and a few grains of rice to propitiate the Goddess and wept at her feet in contrition for her sins. Was the drought then a sequel to Nathan's killing the snake, a black cobra in Rukmani's vines as Kali her friend had foreboded: "It is a pity, your husband killed the snake since cobras are sacred." Nathan could not "worship it while it dug its fangs in my wife." (15) But the snake becomes Rukmani's and Nathan's albatross and the cause of all tribulations.

In *Some Inner Fury*, the anglicized Kitsamy, brother of Mirabai, was no fervent disciple of Hinduism yet, "At any slight to Hinduism, even the slight implicit in the preaching of another religion, it was Kit, who came bristling to its defence; a loyalty, an aversion to interference, perhaps an inherited reverence for his own religion, made him impatient of and hostile to, any who sought to convert its adherents." (154) The Evangelical method of converting Hindus to Christianity with inducements of all sorts were not stemmed by Hindus because of the latent tolerance in their own faith. Kit, despite his western sensitivity, cannot reconcile to these slights to his Hinduism.

In *A Silence of Desire*, Sarojini worshipped the "tulasi" and lit a lamp to it every evening. To her husband Dandekar, an English-educated white-collar job holder, "It was a plant; one did not worship plants." (5) But even in his rationalism he submits "it was a symbol of God, whom one worshipped and it was necessary that God should have symbols since no man had the power or temerity to visualize Him." (5) Dandekar worked with some Indians who had been converted to Christianity. They had a Christian contempt for Indian "heathenism" and ranked the worship of cows or snakes as idolatry but that of printings, prints and statues as worship of God.

Religious controversies in *Possession* centre on spiritualism and materialism. To Caroline, Valmiki's paintings on the cave-walls are in the wilderness hidden from human eye that could see and appreciate it. But the Swamy refutes her charge as "blasphemous": "Where is waste in the work a man does to glorify his God, it is blasphemy to say it." (228) He reminds Caroline of the temples, churches and cathedrals which men have adored and put their all in, though the names of the creators are lost. But Caroline insists that Val's paintings are meant for his eyes alone which the Swamy immediately rebuts: "I am the least, there is also a divine spirit." What are divinations to him are merely artifacts to Caroline.

A Handful of Rice is a clearer exposition of religious differences. To Ravi, Christianity meant little for it hardly impinged on his life. His friend Damodar appears more categorical and vehement in its dismissal as "a spent religion, not only in India where people thought it a bit peculiar but all over the world because it shied away from a contemplation of the immensities of the universe to preoccupy itself with the trivialities of behaviour in this world." (103) Religious dichotomies in India are more pronounced in the urban areas than in the villages. Ravi's father had taught him that Christians were good people and God's neighbours, Ravi does not bear any animosity towards Christianity but is curious about the "coming colours" on the face of the Virgin Mary with the dimpled laughing child Jesus in her arms. He wondered what "could make her look upon her own child with such intimate sadness?"

But there are superstitions galore in the beliefs of some of them. The cartman carrying a collapsed Apu takes it for an evil foreboding. "What evil star had possessed him to carry a man so near death?" he wondered and could not assess what misfortunes might befall his family if the stranger died on his hands. Jayamma, Apu's wife, knowing there was no recovery for Apu lavished faith on charms and amulets in a bid to "thumb defiance at the fate that was forcing them to their knees." Evil spirits warded off by sprinkling rice with small black stones like mustard seeds. Dross superstitions are hopelessly mixed up with religion.

In *The Coffer Dams,* Clinton's distrust of the Indians is based on his conviction that they were "a people who worshipped birds and beasts and probably snakes, decking the forest with scruffy hutches which they knocked up out of driftwood and crammed with leaves and flowers for their deities." (76) But his wife Helen reminds him of their own beliefs like "one does not walk over graves wearing jackboots."

Srinivas in *The Nowhere Man* is only assimilated into his Christian neighbourhood when he participates in Christmas celebrations.

In *Two Virgins,* Amma and Aunt Alamelu are active practitioners of the Hindu faith. They observe rites and rituals with zeal and the Christian teacher Miss Mendoza with suspicion and disdain.

They condemn her for being "a three rupee convert" whose ancestors had converted for monetary benefits. Appa is more rational and explains to little Saroja that it was as easy to enter a Christian Church as it was to enter a Hindu temple. Amma was fastidious about her little prayer room in which pictures were arranged on a wooden platform and decorated. In the centre the "tulasi" was placed in a brass container. Amma did not understand the meaning of the Sanskrit prayers she recited but "one has to prepare before God can enter." After her praying Amma gave spoonfuls of consecrated milk to Lalitha and Saroja. Miss Mendoza too had her symbols. There was "a picture of her God with his chest cut cruelly open. You could not see the chest because of the robes but the heart was revealed. It was neat and trim and ruby-coloured not a bit like the raw hearts you saw in Muslim butcheries." (11) But the heart looked very mild that "didn't foster your faith in miracles. There is such a thing as religious love, it is nearer to ecstasy."

Saroja observed people "surrendering things in the temple, not to each other but to God." Things like fruits, honey, flowers, coconuts and milk were laid at God's feet which Saroja considered good and proper. Garlands of roses and jasmines were also offered while the richer devotees offered gold and silver necklaces set with rubies and diamonds. Appa did not approve of such offerings, insisting that the priests took it for themselves but Amma and Saroja thought such apostasy unwarranted. The Gods they knew were bedecked with jewellery on festival day and then it was all locked away in the temple treasury. Some had to be sold to maintain the temple and feed the poor and the priests. During epidemics men made more offerings but "God was above worldly riches besides having an infinity of his own." So it only enriched the priests. One could make an offering through an emissary but "it was a dreadful sin not to keep your promise to God."

In Miss Mendoza's church too, people offered candles. Lalitha informed Saroja that rich people also gave objects of gold and silver that were kept in a glass case in the crypt.

Despite Appa's rationality, he could not escape the penance for throwing away consecrated coconut, he who Amma said had "no respect for anything; not anything at all, neither God nor man." Appa was made to repent a whole night and in the morning he went to the temple traversing its precincts thrice in bare feet with head covered and carrying a coconut in hand to atone for what he had done. In Miss Mendoza's church, the sacrament of Holy Communion was taken in the mouth: "it was a wafer, it changed miraculously into a slice of God when placed on your tongue." The beliefs are the same in both religions but each mocks the other and lacks respect for it.

Amma fulfils a vow by bathing in the Ganges at Varanasi, burning "camphor in a silver ladle and circling the fame thrice around them to prevent the eye of envy ravaging her beautiful daughters," making her superstitious as well.

In *The Golden Honeycomb,* the British Resident Mr. Buckidge's animosity towards the Brahmin Dewan arises out of the feeling that he considers the other "a devious Hindoo" with as many facets as the faces of "his innumerable gods, which you saw lush and immoderate in his temple." The other Resident's wife, Lady Copeland, engages a Christian ayah who pleases her Christian mistress by calling the gardener's daughter Janaki "a pagan cow." The English community at Devapur is appalled that a religious festival should be so rowdy as a Holi. Bawajiraj II despite his western education believes that charity to beggars will gain him merit. For Mrs. Copeland too, religion enjoins charity as a way of inheriting the Kingdom of heaven. Like Amma of the earlier book, Vatsala too undertakes an annual pilgrimage to the holy city of Kasi.

The first time we meet the holy man in Markandaya is in her third novel *A Silence of Desire.* The Swamy hovers as a nemesis over the entire plot though we never meet him as a person. Sarojini believes firmly that her tumour can only be cured through faith in him. Dandekar's colleague Sastri believes faith-cure to be "the performance of the impossible, the revelation of the divine, mystery and beatitude." (113) Sarojini visits him in her best clothes, pays him tributes out of her little treasures and consequently neglects her home. Dandekar tracks her down to the Swamy's place which he finds guarded by a dwarf. Inside is a motley crowd of social derelicts so that when his friend Sastri asks, "Is he a charlatan? Is it possible that he's genuine?" Dandekar replies slowly, "I don't know. . . . I don't think he's a charlatan. There were a good many people there . . . would they have been there if he was?" The need for the Swamy is voiced by the dwarf: "I don't want my spirit all squashed and twisted like the body you couldn't take your eyes from, that's why?" (157) Dandekar too realized that "when you were with the Swamy . . . nothing material or physical mattered." Material things became worthless trumperies and for a while you found peace, till when you came away the pains, the worry, the misery, the need or craving for wealth returned. Conceding the Swamy's spiritualism, Dandekar still wonders if he can heal Sarojini, but Rajan had been cured by him. Dandekar swings back and forth in his faith but the more pragmatic Ghosh calls the Swamy "a fraud, an impostor, a man who preys on the credulous." The dwarf at his gate is "like those leopards princelings used to keep tied upon the lawn." While he put up an appearance of living in poverty, his store-rooms were crammed with food. And with his claims of spiritual healing he only drew women to himself who paid for illusory cures in cash and kind and any other way he asked them to. He dealt in an atmosphere of drugs, devils, incense. But Chari, the head of the office, remarks that Ghosh's comments are only "to impress the world and prove he's right out in front with the best of the moderns, bombs and all, but no witches, no holy men." Ghosh insists that the Swamy is "fattening on credulous fools" and living off them. The Swamy would soon disappear with his riches leaving the sick behind him. The Swamy does indeed move out because of pressures mounted on him but he goes, Sarojini says, because, "he had no attachments to keep him in this or that place . . . it was the people about him that formed an attachment to him, though it was against all his teaching." (216) His followers have lost their spiritual sustenance. "The Swamy used to hold them up—keep their heads above water." Now their spirits had snapped and their bodies would soon be finished.

In *Possession,* the theme of the holy man is further strengthened. Caroline having brought Valmiki in body cannot possess him in soul. He loses the spiritual inspiration that had sustained his art. It was the Swamy who had by becoming a protector to him and other old and infirm social cast-offs, nurtured him with love and care and proper guidance. He was "a thin muscular figure with not an ounce of spare flesh anywhere, not a stitch of clothing on his body." He had abjured passions and renounced all to live in the wilderness. To Val he becomes indeed a father-figure who has his interests at heart and gives him the address of an "ashram" he can seek shelter in, when in the city. In London Val misses this "father and mother and friend. Always good. Always help." It was not that he lived with the Swamy who was constantly travelling, but when Val needed him he was at hand which Anasuya compares "with the unimpeachable authority of those who have felt the grace of God." Caroline in a bid to make Valmiki work better dupes him with fake letters from the Swamy which Anasuya sees through, knowing that an Indian ascetic, unlike a Christian missionary, does not seek earthly attachments. In Madras Anasuya finds the Swamy surrounded by affluent European women who "craved tranquillity, he embodied it." The Swamy asks her for news of Valmiki confessing that he had not been able to forget him and may have sought the ascetic life too early to crave such an attachment. Valmiki, he says, will always be welcome home because he had realized God, early and "where other men despair, he will turn to God." The Swamy is invited by his new disciples to Kensington and many gifts were made to him which he never used for himself, nor hoarded nor banked but returned the surplus to the giver. To Caroline the Swamy's hold is "a spiritual seduction" and could not be tolerated in England, but ironically it was England that had felt a need of him. Caroline's attitude is compared to that of the Swamy "whose principles of morality were both inflexible and majestic, requiring a scrutiny not only of ends but of means and rejecting as indefensible a plea for lack of knowledge." (144)

Swami Vivekananda explains that when a man has fulfilled his worldly obligations, he must abandon altogether worldly pursuits of possession, fame and power, recognizing the impermanence of these paltry prizes and seek spiritual knowledge by excelling in love and compassion. This is the ideal stage of his life. Markandaya emphasizes the need for this in her novel *The Golden Honeycomb.* Retirement is a known Western concept which is akin to the Hindu renunciation. The Political Agent and the Dewan prepare for retirement according to their own philosophies. One longs for physical relaxation, the Dewan aims for spiritual peace "under a banyan tree . . . a place of stony and monastic character," crumbling with vines splitting the stone work in the silence of which he can recoup his spiritual reserves. Swami Vivekananda writes: "No man who thinks of woman, as his wife can ever perfect be."[19]

Accordingly the Dewan keeps his wife "at one remove" from him but he treats her with courtesy. He is detached from his family and feels less craving for the luxuries of his present existence.

Through all these examples Markandaya has chiefly been concerned with a spirited defence of her own Hindu ideology. She goes into minor details in an effort to explain the rightness of these practices and asserts herself. But that is not all. Artistically, they are used as fosters that mould her character, provide for their strengths and weaknesses.

III

Ruth Prawer Jhabvala approaches philosophical and religious differences between the East and the West in a western perspective and with a comic vision. She has been nurtured on the belief that each man's soul is his alone and has an everlasting quality though it came to him only at birth. Long after the body disintegrates the soul will suffer the consequence of its life on earth, being rewarded for good actions and punished for evil ones. The whole process of transmigration of souls or man's essential divinity are considered blasphemous.

Jhabvala comically observes how the Indian commiserates his present pitfalls and relates them to the evils done or as punishment for the wrongs done in a past life. Radha in *To Whom She Will* and Ram Nath's wife Lakshmi in *Esmond in India* wonder what sins they had committed in being punished in this life in their children's or husband's actions. Ram Nath in *Esmond in India* compares passivity in Indian women to that of cows who never raise a cry even when maltreated. His western education has made him pragmatic enough to tease his wife Lakshmi that she might be punished still more in her next life for not showing respect to her husband. Esmond himself having lived some years in India longs to return to England among its solid grey houses and people where he would not feel constantly dwarfed by the unchanging unending expanse of a meaningless monotony of the Indian sky.

In *The Householder,* Jhabvala jibes fun at those westerners who, tired of their materialism, crave solace and tranquillity in India and wish to lose their individual egos in universality. They get caught in a vortex of pseudo-philosophical vocabulary and feel they are merging with sky and earth in a cosmic energy, by running around the Jantar Mantar. Ironically the householder Prem is struggling to gain material benefits which his American friend Earnest refutes: "Development of the soul. That's the important thing; and India has known it all along and has been 'growing souls' like sky-scrapers and sweet potatoes are grown in western countries, bringing materialism and spiritualism to a single denominator." He seems to understand why India has mortified its beauty, sunsets, tigers, women and songs, all for the development of the soul which teaches universal love. The foreigners get carried away by universal love to mean uninhibited love: "That's what we all need—divine love, spiritual love, every kind of love." (96) Sarla Devi in *Get Ready for Battle* practises universal kinship by working ceaselessly for the slum-dwellers of Bundi Busti. She is placed in direct juxtaposition to her merchant husband Gulzari Lal and her son Vishnu who has also proved to be "a little merchant's son."

Europeans of varied interests are present in *A Backward Place.* Clarissa has been drawn to India through the writings of Vivekananda so that her attitude seems to Sudhir as being "intent on a quest in which notions of soul and God played a prominent if vague part." (117) She kept up the pretence of doing so, becoming more ridiculous and "soul and God perhaps no nearer." But Clarissa feels she has achieved some spirituality: "I've succeeded to some extent. I think I may say that my values are spiritual and not material like that of other Westerners." A person like Etta, she feels, does not deserve to be in India because she does not grasp that "India calls for spiritual adjustments." Clarissa in her bohemian way feels she has given up materialism and to have been able to do so she believes she must have been Indian in all her previous births. The Hochstadts come to India with a scholarly interest in India's philosophy and would like a serious comparative study of Indian and Western spiritual achievements. They themselves have exercised a studied detachment and feel enriched by India, its art, religion and philosophy so indissolubly mixed up as manifestations of the human spirit.

Raymond in *A New Dominion* has come to India as a traveller to learn more about the country with which he had been long associated because of relatives in the Raj. He meets Lee, Margaret and Evie who have come to India on a spiritual quest. Margaret has come to do good to herself, "to learn, to take from India . . . she wants to be pure—to have a pure heart untainted by modern materialism." (26) Attitudes to death are provoked by attitudes towards the soul. To Lee, the dead body tied to a bamboo pallet and covered with a red cloth is horrifying. She accompanies it to the cremation where the smell of charred flesh is strong in her nostrils. The English prefer their dead to lie safely in tombs in the cemetery through which the Christian missionary Miss Charlotte walks Raymond, carefully weeding out the overgrowth to pretty up the place. Raymond is embarrassed at Banubhai the mystic woman claiming his Indian friend Gopi for a son from previous incarnations—in which they had once been queen and prince, a potter's wife and son. Gopi believes this easily and gravitates to Banubhai with the reverence he did not always show his own mother. The new convert Margaret is so zealous in her spiritual excercise that she refuses to be treated by a doctor even when she is seriously ill. She believes, as the Swamy has taught her, that the westerner gets his diseases in India because he tries "to resist India—because we shut ourselves up in our little western egos and don't want to give ourselves."

In *Heat and Dust,* Miss Tietz despite her years in India as a missionary feels that only an immense faith in God can keep one in India because "nothing human means anything here. Not a thing." The neglect of the human body by a European who does not quite understand, has a monkey pick lice out of it. He suffers sickness and disease. The European is horrified by the dirt, squalor and disease and wrongfully attributes it to India's neglect of material being in pursuit of spiritual gains. The missionaries bear with it because of their own hopes of redemption.

The graves of the English were choked with weeds and stripped of all marble railings and adornments after the Raj. Such emblems are meaningless in India; so the angel stood mutilated over the grave of the Saunders's baby.

The young narrator feels that the vast open spaces bring about "a sense of communion" with everything below and above the sky. But the Europeans, in a futile bid to find peace, are misled by lofty misconceptions and wrong notions of spirituality. They feign the ascetic's lifestyle without true renunciation and spout vague philosophies like Chid which are lauded by none but the Indians to whom it seems natural to believe that it is "a very old soul which has passed through many incarnations . . . in India" and has therefore returned to it.

While making mention of this controversial belief, Jhabvala makes ironic references to the way the West seems intent on interpreting India in a quick scanty fashion. The Indian philosophy of reincarnation is not ingrained in the West and adaptation in the true sense was not easy. Jhabvala suggests in her essay "Myself in India" that the "eyes of the spirit" are turned inside because life is so terrible or it is unnecessary to improve perhaps because of its unbearable environment.[20]

In Jhabvala, this Indian attitude is defined as passivity and not stoicism. In *To Whom She Will*, Hari Sahni lacks the courage to submit his intentions of marrying Amrita. He quietly acquiesces to marry a girl chosen by his family in the manner of R.K. Narayan's Malgudi heroes. While preparations for his marriage are in full swing he plans to elope to Europe with Amrita. Instead of calling off his wedding and eloping, Hari Sahni bemoans "the inevitable, the fate-ordained ending to his great love." (186) His passivity becomes more ridiculous when he feels fate has been "a cruel bitter thing . . . that they should be thus torn asunder, that the flood of fate should come rushing between them and carry them away." (278)

In *Esmond in India,* Uma deplores her daughter Gulab and grandchild Ravi's fate that they should be linked to Esmond. She often visits astrologers to find when their times would improve. When her brother, the Cambridge-educated political-idealist, Ram Nath, teases her she says: "You may laugh at these things, but I have had much experience of their truth and greatness. Everything is written in the stars, it is a very ancient science." (159) Man is a victim of time which relates to the planets under which a man is born. Ram Nath's wife Lakshmi shares Uma's belief in the stars. It is written in her son Narayan's horoscope that he will go far in life, even if he was a doctor in the wilds of Madhya Pradesh. Gulab passively bears her English husband Esmond's insults till she is molested by her servant at which point she returns to live with her mother accepting it as "her fate . . . without emotional comment in the way one should accept one's fate." Swami Vivekananda has defined the householder as one who must earn money with great effort and enthusiasm to support his family in comfort, failing which there can be no *Moksha* for him.[21] The householder who struggles to become rich by good means and for good purposes is doing practically the same thing for the attainment of salvation as the anchorite does in his cell when he is praying. Against this, Jhabvala's portrait of Prem is comic irony. Prem cannot and does not take action to improve his finances and is indeed passive in his role.

Sarla Devi in *Get Ready for Battle* does not battle with the circumstances of her life; she accepts her fate and rises above it to involve herself in social work.

In *A Backward Place,* Judy has in many ways adopted herself to life in India but she has her moments of doubt. Bhuaji by contrast has a ready acceptance of all that life gives. She believes that God provides. Judy had "a kind of easy faith that someone . . . would provide, and that when the time came, everything always worked out." (78) Bhuaji accepted all as "God's will" and one's ups and downs were a matter of time as "life takes us here and there." Judy did not want to give up what she had: "She was determined to hold on tight to what she had, like her mother, like her Aunt Agnes, like all those other stubborn dwellers in little houses among whom she had grown up and who, she now decided, were her kind." (219)

In *A New Dominion,* Lee notes at first how the Indians accepted the overcrowding in the bus, its ensuing heat and smells and discomfort without question. She learned to accept them because she wanted to "lose herself." Seeing some of the terrible sights in India, she had "begun to accept the fact that it was the fate of many to suffer hunger and disease." This sense of resignation seemed to creep on Europeans who had stayed long enough in India. In quietly accepting to be married, Gopi in *A New Dominion* is like Hari Sahni in *To Whom She Will.* Only "those with an unpropitious fate had to drag through life unmarried and uncared for." So, Gopi allows himself to be "taken over" by "his fate" in the form of relatives. Raymond does not understand why Gopi cannot decide against it if he has doubts. The idea of acceptance reaches a horrifying climax in the story of the dog that is left to die at the *ashram* gates. Lee wants to put it to death to ease its agony but the Swami opines, "everything must be experienced to the end. This is true for a dog as for a man as for a bird on a tree. Everything must unfold and ripen. . . . We must accept and enjoy or accept and endure, as the case may be. Because we need both enjoyment and endurance, both sun and storm so that we may ripen into our fullest possibility . . . even a dog should be allowed to grow into such ripeness. And if for a dog, then how much more for a human being." (181) Lee is confused and distressed because she thinks it is in conflict with the Swami's precepts of universal love.

In *Heat and Dust,* the young narrator meets a missionary whose long years in India have wrought a change in her attitude to life. She has lived only in His will and will do only as He wills. But Inder Lal, she finds, is resigned to his wife's illness and his work at the office. The general lethargy in the "Heat and Dust" of India are all emanations of resignation and quiet acceptance. No voices protest at the state of affairs in hospitals, municipalities and other deplorable conditions in India. Like the dog in *A New Dominion,* the beggar woman is left dying on a refuse dump uncared for.

Jhabvala writes in "Myself in India" that an "approach to India's basic conditions is to accept them . . . an approach favoured by most Indians." But even though the Indian climate invites one to be passive and resigned, Europeans like herself after a time resent "being sucked down into that bog of passive, intuitive being."[22] She redeems her cynicism with comic irony in her stories. But in her later stories, her western alacrity and egoistic beliefs cleave through with an irritability at such a confounded way of thinking. Her long years in India sometimes make her resigned like Judy, only slightly fidgety; at other times like Etta and Esmond she wants to break out of her air-conditioned status to free thinking and living.

Jhabvala again studies the Indian religion against what Swami Vivekananda says are the cardinal features of the Hindu religion[23]—meditative and speculative philosophy and the ethical teachings contained in the various books of the Vedas. In *Esmond in India*, Uma finds sustenance in her religion. She takes recourse to prayer specially when disturbed. Her maid Bachani recounts to Gulab, Uma's daughter, that "All morning she prayed . . . she would not talk with anyone. Afterwards she went down to the Jumna to bathe, and how she prayed as she sprinkled water!" (22) At night she sang hymns for two hours with Swamiji playing the harmonium. In her present concern for her daughter, she "could speak only to God, no one else knows what moves in a mother's soul." Uma compares her actions with those of Arjuna in the battle of Mahabharata where intense activity is espoused in eternal calmness. It achieves a mock-epic seriousness which the author's satirical mode encourages, making Uma forget the more important of that premise—calmness. Uma requests Shakuntala to paint for her "a beautiful picture of Siva-Parvati for my prayer-room" before whom "what respect can any of us claim, when before Him we are all smaller than the smallest of all insects." (237) She undertakes prayers and fasts and is often heard quoting the *Gita*.

Prem's mother in *The Householder* offered "special prayer" for Prem, to "bring blessings to this house, for your service." The fruits and flowers she offered at his feet are given to Prem's wife Indu.

Sarla Devi in *Get Ready for Battle* was a deeply religious woman and would take her son Vishnu to many a prayer-meeting where they sang hymns together. Her life is one of penance and prayer but, unlike Uma in *Esmond in India,* one of active social work.

In *A Backward Place,* Bhuaji is a very pious woman who said many prayers, visited the temple often and took her purificatory dips in the river, not only because other people might be looking but because she derived satisfaction from it and liked and needed it. Judy on the other hand "had brought with her from England an ingrained mistrust of the pious." These instinctive reactions had become modified through her contact with Bhuaji. Judy is coaxed by Bhuaji to take the blessings of a holy man who is believed to have great powers. She can see that in Bhuaji's temple many widows and "a few young married ones, many pregnant, reverentially carried fresh green leaves and rose petals." India's deeply religious character is fascinating to the westerner only so far as he does not permit his consciousness of India's reality to permeate that.

In *A New Dominion,* Lee and Margaret are at first inhibited about singing with gay abandon. They are stiff and shy, locked in their egos. Gradually they are able to merge with the rest of the congregation. Raymond observes how at Benares, Hindu widows live in prayer and penance; boats went up and down with people chanting prayers to the setting sun and floating little paper boats loaded with candles and flowers in the Ganges. To Raymond, it is a dirty river where crowds of dirty diseased people come to taka a dip and half-burned dead bodies are also thrown in. He wonders how such a polluted river can purify anything. He sees Bulbul's "little clay gods . . . painted and smiling . . . an oleograph of Ganesh the elephant-headed god mounted on his rat" as some folk art. Serious conflict arises over how Margaret's dead body should be treated—be cremated according to Hindu rites because she had been practising Hinduism, or a Christian burial since she was born a Christian. Concerned over a Christian soul, Miss Charlotte takes charge, prepares the body for burial and recites Christian prayers. Lee finds relief in joining Miss Charlotte in those prayers and sat kneeling till Margaret was taken away. Lee had dabbled in Hinduism like Margaret—the latter had died in the process, Lee was saved from the disasters of adopting something that was alien to her spirit. Religious controversy attains symbolic proportions. Asha the ex-princess is also moved by the Christian prayers: "all religions are the same, don't you think so Lee?" but that may be because Hinduism is tolerant of all religions.

In *Heat and Dust,* Jhabvala seems to transpose her own experiences of the feel of religion in India in everyday life on to the young English narrator. Like Jhabvala herself in "Myself in India," the young narrator wakes up to the sound of temple-bells in Satipur. She is not allowed entry into the Nawab's mosque at Khatm and finds instead a shrine put up by the watchman, of Hanuman in a glass case, made of plaster of paris and "dressed in bits of silk and pearl necklaces." She is anxious to get out of the stifling atmosphere with crowds gathered inside accustomed no doubt to high vaults and stained glass windows of magnificent churches. The inner recesses of Hindu shrines are contrasted with the church's lofty dimensions. She also tips out of the bus window the sticky bits of rock sugar and a few flowers she was given at the shrine. She gets another eerie feeling when taken to see the suttee shrines. Inder Lal's mother on the other hand joined her hands in prayer and decorated them with strings of flowers. On certain days she with other women would reverence the shrines for what Dr. Saunders considered "plain savagery and barbarism," for allowing "gruesome, and horrible mutilations in the name of religion."

Mixed up with religion are superstitions. Inder Lal's wife, when possessed by an evil spirit, is not taken to a doctor and the evil spirits are doused by Inder Lal's mother encircling a fistful of rice around the girl's head and cracking her knuckles murmuring some incantation. The English boy Chid, who is experimenting with

Hinduism, asserts that evil spirits must be driven out by applying a red hot iron to the arms and legs. The holy woman advises a pilgrimage for all worries and desires, "a long, long journey high up in the Himalayas." The cool pure fresh mountain air curbs the frail human egos that linger in diseases. Faith drew crowds to the tomb of Baba Firdaus on the festival of "Pati-ki-shadi" and Hindu women made offerings to be cured of childlessness.

In Olivia's story, the Nawab's mother is seen consulting the stars before a journey. When the young narrator is pregnant she comes to the holy woman for abortion, just as Olivia had gone to crude midwives for her abortion. But the narrator sees in Maji a symbol of the goddess of destruction, one who holds "life and death in one hand and plays them like a yo-yo," which makes her change her mind.

Jhabvala's treatment of the Swamy is opposite to that of Markandaya. Jhabvala sees little piety in him, no abstemiousness but a wily charlatan duping gullible Hindus and Christians alike with false promises.

In *Esmond in India* the Swami has been in Uma's big house for nine long years, sitting in orange robes and eating with great relish and appetite from a brass tray. His meals were sent very punctually to him and he sang his hymns lustily to harmonium music. Uma found him a great spiritual comfort and would often discuss with him the doubts in her mind: "But for discussing a specific problem . . . he was not really satisfactory . . . he would talk very wisely and very very spiritually, but always in the abstract, in large philosophical terms." (98) Uma enjoyed the devotional songs and the Swami "so holy and good," playing the harmonium with his eyes cast up to heaven but it did not bring her any long-lasting peace.

Ram Nath's friend Har Dayal had given nothing of his wealth during the freedom struggle and none for spiritual comfort either. He is tormented by the latter and wonders if he can even gain spiritual satisfaction. He finds his life as having gone waste. Only Narayan is a *karma-yogi* in the true sense working conscientiously without an eye on material rewards. The *Gita* specifies that earthly pleasures are only sources of sorrow but Har Dayal's family, even Ram Nath's sister Uma and wife Lakshmi, are pursuing that alone. "After such knowledge, what forgiveness."[24] Jhabvala seems to query.

In *The Householder,* the Europeans's efforts at seeking spiritual solace by awakening the *Kundalini* and meditating become a matter of ridicule. It is not easy to understand renunciation and meditation in its true light, for it does not involve merely parting with physical comforts. It is a matter of surrendering the spirit forever; that is why renunciation and meditation become a frustrating experience to those westerners who experiment with it.

Sarla Devi in *Get Ready for Battle* has made some progress on the path of renunciation, bearing alike "pleasure and pain," but love for her son still draws her to him. Bhuaji in *A Backward Place* has also started on the way to spiritual salvation, undeterred by deficient physical comfort. Clarissa conversely gives up caring for her body by avoiding personal hygiene alone. She cannot and is not chastened by it so that her bath in Mrs. Kaul's bathroom becomes symbolic of her return to normal life.

In *A New Dominion,* Miss Charlotte of the Mission lives a spartan life, dedicating herself to the sick, despite India's daunting conditions of sickness and heat. Margaret, Lee and Evie abandon their beliefs and search out a Swamy. Margaret believes her "inner eyes" have been opened by the Swamy. But Lee was coaxed by him to give facts of all the people she knew, because the different sorts of people at the *ashram* with their different problems soon lost their egos and discovered how trivial each was. It was actually a ploy to gain contact with the ex-princess and her brother Rao Sahib-turned politician. He was clever to set up his *ashram* outside Benares so that new souls could be inspired with a new spirit. But he had ready plans for expansion in the most modern way, and made the present discomforts seem as if they were actually designed by him to break his disciples in endurance. The girl Evie's relations with the Swamy are made ambiguous though ostensibly she is helping him on his sacred treatise. The Swamy was actually devising plans to visit abroad and enjoyed his drinks and non-vegetarian meals with

Raymond while the girl Evie abstained. He explains that it is only when you have given up all enjoyment so that it is no longer enjoyment can you have these things back again. Margaret tries to master her "mantra" for meditation which instead of making her serene makes her taciturn. Lee has a harrowing sexual experience with the Swamy. Margaret falls a prey to jaundice which the Swamy insists on curing with magical powders so that Margaret finally dies. The mystic woman sums up the predicament of the westerner vis-a-vis the Swamy: "foreigners come to India because they are bred in the West. They pretend to be in search of spiritual values but because they don't know what true spiritual values are, they fasten themselves on to harmful elements who only help to drive them deeper down into their disturbed egos." (173)

In *Heat and Dust,* a young English boy and his girl come to India because they are attracted to Hinduism by discourses in England heard from a visiting Swamy. Perhaps the Swamy of *A New Dominion* had finally gone abroad. But in India they do not discover universal love, only dysentery. The English boy who adopted the ascetic's life was given the Indian name of Chidananda, soon shortened to Chid. He forsook his worldly possessions, lost some in thefts, and went around with his beads and a begging bowl. Chid had made a physical renunciation of sorts but he still erased sexual gratification. He ate food thrown to him by people who believed that giving doles to the ascetic gained them credit. He sets off on a pilgrimage to the snowy mountains but finds it impossible to live in cheap hotels. He kept writing home for money and soon contracted dysentery. He tired of everything Indian. Chid had learnt to mouth philosophy and is even heard but as the narrator suggests he has probably pieced scraps of knowledge together. Chid's is a case of disillusionment and frustration.

If the Swamy has been one more factor in her other novels, he becomes central to her latest book *Three Continents*. Michael, like a tragic hero, falls prey to the falsities of the Rawul, the Rani and Crishi chiefly because of his own vulnerability. The scene of action has shifted first to America, then to England and lastly to India, but the idea germane to her earlier novels persists. Of affluent background and good lineage, Michael is ready material for the vultures of spirituality. He has had occasion to travel to the Middle-East and far East for holidays with a grandfather who held ambassadorial assignments. But even though they have "what people would say . . . was pretty good," the twins Michael and Harriet Wishwell are yearning for something more. They suffer from the ills of a materialistic society; a broken home, divorced parents seeking in vain more satisfying relationships in numerous philanderings. They both drop out of college eventually but it is Michael who does so first and sets out in quest of an emotional sustenance or "the real thing." He resists the usual abodes of "hippies"—Kathmandu, Gangtok, Buddh Gaya and Goa. But it is in Delhi that he encounters the dubious Crishi in a seedy hotel they are both occupying, very near a Hindu temple. Crishi, like Iago, is wicked from the start but Michael is blind to it. When they meet again, in a fashionable quarter in London, Crishi is transformed into a nattily-dressed gentleman stepping out of an art-dealer's store, and preparing to step into a limousine. At first he hardly recognizes the "hippie" Michael, but when he accidentally lets it be known that he has ambassadorial connections, the scoundrel Crishi latches on to him with the Rawul, the Rani and the entire entourage. "Propinquity" is the launching-pad for their entrance into wealthy American society and they take over the place as if it belonged to them. The Rawul with his age and deportment provides their organization a spiritual front. To him it was a grandiose idea that he be constituted the saviour of world civilization. Harriet's observation that "a modest man as the Rawul could have such an exalted notion of himself" is really understanding the concept of renunciation that attaches itself to spiritual men. Their whole lifestyle is contrary to the western concepts of renunciation. The Rawul's relations with the Rani are suspect; in turn hers with Crishi are questionable and the whole entourage, waiting upon them and vying with each other to serve Rawul's personal needs brings about this realization in the dispassionate observer, Harriet, "that involvement in a higher cause did not so much still the lower passions as stir them up and bring them to a pitch."

Only the Rawul's speeches seem to hold his listeners under a mesmeric spell, as he holds forth on orations of a fourth World—a world free of all its ills and limitations. Right from the start, it is evident that the group is really out to have "Propinquity." Michael believes this to be "the real thing" and not "niti," a word the twins have substituted in their private jargon, for phoney. It is Michael's naivete that brings on his disaster. But he is sold enough to their duplicity and declares to Harriet, "This is it Harriet, *Om* the real thing." On this front, Harriet holds and even after she marries Crishi and travels with the "Family" to London. There she encounters the Rawul's family, the Bari Rani and their three daughters, all living and believing in opulence—a far cry from the asceticism that associates with spiritual beings. Even an old guard like the Babaji in London owns a huge mansion that is sold to the Rawul. Even on his sick-bed he was attracted to this American girl and confessed to having mesmerized many like her in her earlier days. Only his knowledge seemed profounder than the Rawul's, another indication of the latter's hoax. Harriet has heard him respect "Adhibhantika" and "Adhyatmika" in a later lecture. If the Babaji had discoursed on "transcendentalism," the Rawul extends it to "transcendental internationalism" which will make "a heaven on earth."

In her inimitable way, Jhabvala makes her subtle satiric comment on what passes for spirituality. It is the weak-willed West that becomes a prey willy-nilly to such hoax, the stranger and stouter of spirit, will declare as Michael does at the end of it all, that the Rawul is all "bunk."

IV

From an examination of their novels it is clear that Markandaya and Jhabvala are both conscious of their parent philosophies and religion and well-acquainted with those of the land of their adoption. But it is not merely to display their knowledge of the two philosophies and religions that they make consistent use of it in their books. It would be more in order to suggest that their own tugs and pulls of the two divergent views have found an outlet in their work. Each is conscious of the innate beliefs of the parent religion and philosophy and find it difficult to compromise with the other but compromise they do, or else we would have found a more categorical negation or affirmation as the case may be. But the issue is left mid-air after both sides have made their points or through a character who displays tolerance and compassion emulating the extreme views. Their purpose in the novels is manifold. In Markandaya we found that each character is moulded to the framework of his religious and philosophical beliefs. Those more exposed to western pragmatism and rationalism are scientific in their approach yet rooted in their traditional beliefs from which, despite their knowledge, they find they cannot sever links. The drama is not only with outside forces but within him also, such a case is that of Dandekar in *A Silence of Desire*.

The rooted traditionalism in Indians is apparent in Rukmani in *Nectar in a Sieve*. She personifies the stoicism and fortitude that draws its strength from Indian religion and philosophy and which western pragmatism and hard-boiled logic has done its best to undermine. Rukmani emerges as the heroine of the novel because she surmounts everything that is aimed at weakening her integrity. At the end of the book she compromises, accepts that western science can find a release for Puli's infirmity but only as far as that, no further. When any Indian has wanted to break away wholly he suffers depredation and erosion of character, like Ravi in *A Handful of Rice*. *The Coffer Dams* treats the subject with a certain quality of symbolism. The opinions of the Indians become symbolic of India's new self-respect and assertion when politically free. It signifies a complete break which Helen the English woman contradicts as not being necessary if there is understanding. *The Nowhere Man* uses these philosophical views as manifestations of the expatriates's dilemma. It becomes once again psychological, the battle within him as much as without. In *Two Virgins*, it is used to divide the two camps of East and West more specifically. Here again a certain amount of symbolism is interjected in the innuendo that India's culture and religion were also assaulted by Britain.

Lalitha's abortion is symbolic of the fact that the East and the West cannot be married fruitfully, if the union be forced. There was need to overcome many hurdles. Taken together, Markandaya's handling of religious and philosophical differences appear as a metaphor for her opinion that India has withstood outside interference for centuries on her religion and philosophy, only because of its strength. It has lent her the moral timber to emerge victorious after all. Those who try to break away, either cannot do so or are thereby redeemed only after they have paid a price for it like Valmiki in *Possession*. *The Golden Honeycomb* showed that it could still stand and must do so instead of compromising with the West which could only end in disaster, like Lalitha's prostitution in *Two Virgins*. We could still be, like Saroja, chastened by our experience. This helps make her work literature.

Jhabvala too has brought to her work an expatriate's dilemma. In her first novels she has only taken a comic vision exposing the hypocrisies between what they profess and what they do. She finds that western consciousness cannot compromise with the general lethargy and apathetic attitude because the principles of renunciation are not embedded in it. But comic vision is charged with vehemence in the later novels suggesting her own difficulties of merging with India. She does not think it at all possible that a European can adopt Indian beliefs and be at peace. There will always be some frustration, a disillusionment at the end, corroborating Markandaya's contention that the East and the West cannot meet as friends, at least not yet. There are numerous differences—religion and philosophy are amongst them. They provide a dramatic content to her stories but also a psychological insight into her characters. We find them struggling, trying hard to grasp at something but on coming nearer they are drawn back. About the holy men Jhabvala is apparently in agreement with Christophor Isherwood that "the Swami is associated with theatrical trickery . . . the West quite unaware that those who have the right to call themselves by it have taken monastic vows; that it is in fact a little just as worthy of respect as that of 'father' in the Catholic Church."[25] Jhabvala is confirmed in her opinion that Swamis are humbug and motivated by commercial interests rather than spiritual ones.

These charlatans dupe the westerners who are surfeited by their own materialism and some wealthy Indians too. She appears intrigued that western rationality does not see through such duplicity.

The general body of their novels makes religious and philosophical differences a major deterrent to a lasting relationship between the East and the West. It is in the psyche and spirit of the two peoples which no hasty coming together can overcome successfully. It is not that they are pessimistic in their outlook; rather optimistic that with care, understanding and love can be affected in a more permanent solution. The quick attempts can only end in disaster as they do in "encounters" in their novels. This understanding of men and the matters of their heart makes their work a literature of concern for humanity and in that they have been successful.

NOTES

1. Thompson, *An End of the Hours*, p.137.
2. Heinrich Zimmer, *Myths and Symbols in Indian Art and Civilization* (New York, 1946), p. 21
3. Heinrich Zimmer, *The Philosophies of India* (New York, 1951), p. 45.
4. Swami Vivekananda *The Teachings of Swami Vivekananda* (Calcutta: 1971), IV, p. 191.
5. Heinrich Zimmer, *The Philosophies of India*, pp. 43-44.
6. Basil Mitchell, ed., *The Philosophy of Religion* (O.U.P. 1971), p. 78.
7. Swami Vivekananda, IV, pp. 188-189.
8. D. Ramakrishna, ed., *Indian English Prose*.
9. Percival Spear, *A History of India*, 2, p. 122.
10. Swami Vivekananda, III, pp. 45-46.
11. See S. Radhakrishnan, *East and West: Some Reflections* (London, 1954).
12. Heinrich Zimmer, *The Philosophies of India*, p. 100.

13. K.R. Srinivas Iyenger, p. 31.
14. *Ibid.*, p. 162.
15. *Ibid.*, p. 312.
16. Margaret P. Joseph, p. 214.
17. Swami Vivekananda, III, p. 198.
18. S. Radhakrishnan, p. 24.
19. Swami Vivekananda, IV, p. 394.
20. Ruth Prawer Jhabvala, *How I Became a Holy Mother and Other Stories*, p. 15.
21. Swami Vivekananda, V, pp. 448-49.
22. Ruth Prawer Jhabvala, *How I Became a Holy Mother and Other Stories*, p. 10.
23. Swami Vivekananda, II, p. 292.
24. T.S.Eliot, "Gerontion," *Selected Poems* (Faber, Bristol, 1970), p. 32.
25. *Teachings of Swami Vivekananda*, Introduction by Christopher Isherwood (Pithoragarh), p. xvii.

The Socio-Cultural Economic Encounter

The social historian T.G. Percival Spear has traced the beginnings of a social rift between the English and the Indians to a later period in their social history.[1] He claims that the Sahib in India during the hey-day of the East India Company behaved in an affable manner, when not rapaciously concerned with improving his financial status. He often married and adopted the local inhabitants's art of living. Trade with the Indians had brought him to deal with the native on a par. But with the growth of the Company's dominions and their takeover by the Crown, the role of the Englishman was reversed. He came to India without fear or favour. He believed that the majority of them were afflicted with the traditional Eastern vices of trickery, dishonesty, lechery, fecklessness and inefficiency. He himself was influenced by the Evangelical Movement which promoted the idea of Christian superiority of faith. Possessed of this superiority complex, the English excluded the Indians from their social sphere. Not being engaged in trade they saw no reason to mix with the local inhabitants. The situation was further aggravated by their women. Mr. Kincaid cites the example of one Mrs. Lushington who had asked a senior lady what she had seen of the country and its people since her first coming to India and the latter had replied: "Oh nothing, thank goodness. I know nothing at all about them, no I don't wish to. I think the less one knows of them the better." The British idea of superiority of their race bred contempt for intermarriage as well as its products. They strictly adhered to their own way of life.

Indian society had been a changeless one based in the village community. Romila Thapar elucidates how with the prevailing caste system, "each man . . . had its own role in the large and more complex network of the social structure."[3] Man's ultimate destiny lay in the transcendence of the soul to spiritual salvation so that the requirements of his social life were only of transitory value. Each one's right to spiritual peace was recognized and there was a need to harmonize man and nature. Such metaphysical thinking encouraged at the same time a withdrawal from life and from social institutions devised at a purposeful ordering of life. The Indians associated life lived against this natural background with qualities of gentleness, truthfulness while the West interpreted it as passivity, other-worldliness. The Indians maintained that their culture had an essentially spiritual quality and was therefore superior to the materialism of the West. Its art was upheld as being more authentic because it expressed spiritual values as against the Greek art of the West that was obsessed with physical beauty. The English on the other hand found Indian art unaesthetic and unappealing.

But what irked the wealthy European most was that India was "on the back of this great animal of poverty and backwardness,"[3] and the wealthy Indian's apathy to it. The Indian economy had been broad-based before the advent of the English. But the imposition of English goods and English tax laws drove Indian crafts out of business so that they all returned to the village and agriculture. The land was owned by the new landed-gentry, and the peasant worked on it and paid taxes. Bad harvests and poor irrigational facilities impoverished the peasant to a degree he has still to recover from.

The impact of the West on the Indian mind gradually wrought changes on the Indian mind in attitude and ideology. India had many of the cultural conditions favourable to the novel before she came into contact with Europe. But it was with the introduction of English education in which a large section of Indians were brought up within the spectrum of this new and enlightened education that a chain of action and reaction set in, providing the stuff that novels are made of. Tagore made the first effort to create a new culture by fusing the East and the West together in his *Gora* in 1923. The thread was soon caught up by subsequent writers of the Indian milieu whose major concern it became to see how the East and the West came together.

In the novels of the thirties and the forties at the height of the freedom struggle the writers's attitudes were mostly biased against the Britisher; bitter memories associated with the British rule overshadowed the pleasant experiences with individual Englishmen. Mulk Raj Anand caricatured English in *Two Leaves and a Bud* and R.K. Narayan found the Englishmen insufferably proud of their economic and intellectual superiority in *The English Teacher*. This bitterness disappeared in the fifties. The hold of traditions was gradually relaxing while a new culture born of the clash between the East and the West was merging imperceptibly but decisively. The large audience of the educated class was questioning the age; old social dogmas and society were being re-interpreted with their new-found knowledge. The Indian novelist today works mainly against this background. Indian society has always been a group-society in which the atomization of the West is still foreign. The drama in these novels unfolds in the broad social content in which one life reflects another. One sees this in the tensions between the new urbanized class and their village kinsmen; between minority groups and those who still seek to uphold monolithic barriers between the masses and those in public office, between the young and their middle-aged parents and guardians.

Markandaya and Jhabvala have seen India at close quarters and have acquired an intimate understanding of its ideas, ideals and various modes of life. They are as well-acquainted with Western ideals and mode of life. The major theme of their novels is the social, cultural, economic clash of these two modes, the Western and the Oriental. A closer study of their novels will help further elucidation.

II

Kamala Markandaya's acquaintance with Indian life is as authentic as her understanding of the Englishmen and their character. She spent a few years studying the life of South Indian peasants before marrying an Englishman and settling down in London. Culture being ingrained in the personality of the nation, it is visible

not only in domestic habits or sartorial concerns but also in beliefs and convictions. Markandaya's major theme has been the cultural clash of the two modes of life she has seen so closely. The Indian mind was dominated by the feeling that the English mind was pragmatic and the Indian idealistic, and that England was the exploiter and India the exploited. A gradual shift in values and a new angle of vision was wrought by British contact which in many ways proved delectable. India can now be said to be poised delicately between a nostalgic idealization of traditional values and a new compulsive urge for modernity between which she must choose. Should she allow herself to be swamped by the rising tide of Western materialism or resuscitate older concepts of spiritual contentment and self-abnegation?

In *Nectar in a Sieve*, her first novel, this dichotomy of values is captured in a most compelling way. It is the lot of Nathan and Rukmani to till the land belonging to another, paying an exorbitant rent for it and getting hardly a square meal a day as reward even after the best harvest. But Rukmani is content to live in the soulful quietude of her little village till this Garden of Eden is ravaged by a serpent in the form of the tannery. Like marauders, the towns people came with cart-loads of bricks, stones and cement to build this hideous superstructure while their supervisor directed the operations "with loud voice and many gestures but doing not a stroke of work himself." (26) The proprietor, "the red faced whiteman" does not live in the village and only "came and went," thus laying the foundations of an industrial society based on the principles of exploitation of labour and absenteeism. The tannery began to rear its ugly head devouring green open spaces, polluting the clean wholesome atmosphere and tempting simple gullible peasants into greed, ambition and immorality. Some like Kunthi are jubilant at the change and consider "the tannery . . . a boon to us." She asks Rukmani: "Are you not glad that our village is no longer a clump of huts but a small town? Soon there will be shops and tea-stalls even a bioscope." (29) Rukmani's spirit however revolts against this deflowering of pristine innocence. Her intuitive perceptions warn her against the impending disasters and she knows that

the tannery does not augur well for the village. She cried: "They may live in our midst but I can never accept them, for they lay their hands upon us and we are turned from tilling to barter, and hoard our silver since we cannot spend it, and see our children go without the goods, that their children gorge and it is only in the hope that one day things will be as they were that we have done these things." (28) But like a mythical demon the whole village is devoured by the tannery that turns it into a spiritual wasteland: "It is all noise and crowds everywhere and rude young hooligans idling in the street and dirty bazaars and uncouth behaviour and no man thinks of another but schemes only for his money." (46)

The actuation of the painful process of modernization is manifested in the disturbance beyond redemption of the prelapsarian peace of the village. The village is transformed into a small town. Rukmani's own daughter Ira is forced into prostitution by the inexorable laws of neccssity and destitution. Rukmani cries in utter despair: "our money buys less and less. As for living in a town—if town this is why there is nothing I would fly sooner from it if I could go back to the sweet quiet of village life." (46) Soaring prices and greed urge the villagers to demand higher wages and when denied and thwarted they threaten to create trouble for their employers. This builds up menacing tension all over the village. The ravage caused by drought or by excessive and unseasonable rain leads the former to the brink of starvation so that he must sell his possessions like vessels and clothes to pay the rent. Insecurity and privation, however harrowing by themselves, are not the greatest calamities suffered by the landless farmer. When the land he tills is taken away from him so that he is forced to leave the village, it is the ultimate in social inequality and economic disparity that has arisen out of the Western system of intermediary landholders. Rukmani and Nathan are forced to break stones in the quarry outside the city. They know nothing of this job and can only make a pittance. Their lot as urban poor is as pitiable as their life in rural India. Their two sons have left as indentured labourers for Ceylon and another one had come to the city in quest of a job and it is to that El Dorado that Rukmani and Nathan now make their way. India's grinding poverty affects the westerner most of all though it is the West that is in many ways responsible for it. Even Kenny tells Rukmani that he would return to his country when tired of India's follies and stupidities, "your eternal shameful poverty." (71)

One of these stupidities is the social structure in India. Rukmani is reluctant to let her sons work in the tannery, a Western creation, because they are not of the "caste of tanners." She is duly worried about what her relatives will say. Kenny ponders over this: "One goes from one end of the world to the other to hear the same story. Does it matter what people say?" For Rukmani it does. She tells Kenny: "It is easy for you, but perhaps not quite so simple for us." It is therefore important for Rukmani to find a good match for her daughter Ira but the choice is limited by the demands of dowry. Ira's wedding has its share of religion, music, noise and feasting but it does not ensure happiness for Ira. She is rejected by her husband for being barren. The Western method of selecting one's own partner is also not successful as Kenny's divorce from his wife proves. Human nature is same everywhere and Kenny misses his sons just as Nathan does his.

In *Nectar in a Sieve* the relations between the East and the West are generally friendly but mutual inability to comprehend the motivation and behaviour of the other remains a common problem.

Markandaya's next novel *Some Inner Fury* presents India against the backdrop of the freedom movement of 1942, caught in the maelstrom of her struggle against British rule. The younger generation provoked by constant humiliation and repression rises against both, foreign domination and parental tutelage. The atmosphere is electrified by this revolution that is at once political and social. Mirabai the young protagonist of the novel is born of rich though orthodox parents. But flushed with a new sense of independence she falls in love with the Governor's military aide—Richard Marlowe. The liaison with an Englishman is itself a rude assault on "the powerful and seemingly impregnable citadel of convention." Despite her mother's admonition that "it is not right for a young woman to go among young men," (38) Mira rides roughshod over all social taboos and inhibitions. She goes with her lover on a long pre-marital honeymoon in utter disregard of decorum and propriety. Only political and national barriers sunder the relationship to divide them into "your people and my people."

Roshan Merchant is another such emancipated young lady, Oxford-educated and divorced. She too is torn between the cultural and social demands of East-West orthodoxy and non-conformism. "Born in one world, educated in another," she moved in both worlds with ease and nonchalance. She went to dances and parties in lacquered slippers and bright-coloured saris. Both Indians and Englishmen were eager to partner her. Mira and Roshan are members of a newly-emergent society in which "youngmen in Western clothes and English accents . . . flaunted their unorthodoxy and a few girls with shingled hair and advanced views aired them." Entrenched against these angry young people is tradition which wields subtler weapons to vanquish and befuddle its opponent. When Kitsamy returns from Oxford, still in the hold of Western culture,"its brazen ways, its painted women, its easy morality," he is manoeuvred into a prearranged liaison with a girl of his mother's choice. Premala is let loose on him till he capitulates willingly. Premala's mother, explains the novelist, "readily understood the need for this strange new pattern of courtship, deplorable no doubt, but what the times demanded." (51) The marriage is solemnized with the customary ostentation. An Indian marriage is primarily a solemn religious rite, a tradition on which the older generation has been brought up. Premala appeals to Mira's mother for such a marriage, partly because she is traditional in many ways unlike the emancipated Mira. She prefers to sit at Kit's feet and feels a little uncomfortable in Kit's house that he has done up solely in the Western style. His parents's house had been equipped to cope with both Europeans and Indians with "two dining rooms, two kitchens, even two sets of servants." Premala would have preferred to have the same because "parents . . . prefer their own ways." (97) She misses her home with so many people in it; like any Indian home it sheltered her widowed aunt, Dodamma, who had shorn head and wore no blouse under her sari but contributed to the housekeeping by supervising the servants. When Kit's foster-brother Govind comes suddenly on an evening Premala is joyous and welcomes him in the traditional way of a homecoming with a tray laden with small cups of curd, fruit, nuts and sliced copra. Only the betel-leaves were missing. Even the westernized Kit had missed "our food . . . I've only just realised how much." (18)

If Mira and Kit belong to an upper-class family where there is plenty of food left after the meals, outside, hungry children kept vigil waiting to pounce on any crumb which may be had: "they waited, watchful even while they played, brown wily urchins with the warped bodies of perpetual hunger, and the bright uncomplaining eyes of children who somehow contrive to ignore it." (62) When Mira's and Richard's car breaks down, a crowd of beggars surround the car "pressing their demands with increasing vigour." (92) Roshan the journalist in the pitch of India's struggle for freedom, campaigns to improve the conditions in India because of British apathy to slow trains "with no provision for water; of travelling on the footboards, because there was no room anywhere else, or jammed in with a hundred people in a carriage meant for half that number." (119)

In *A Silence of Desire* Dandeker is a "second generation city dweller" working as a clerk in a government department. His contact with the Europeans has no doubt given him a pragmatic and scientific outlook on life. But at heart he remains an Indian who prefers to sit on a mat at home and is convention-bound. The other side of him, his rationality, is shocked to discover that his wife is seeking some kind of faith-cure for a serious ailment. Equally disturbing to him is her idolatrous worship of the *tulasi* plant, yet his deep-rooted traditionalism feels the beauty and potency of her uncompromising faith: "He had been at pains to bring up children, with a correct understanding of these matters and to educate his wife. Not that she did not understand; her religious tutelage had been rather more earnest than his own and she often had answers to the conundrums which his less-amiable, non-Hindu friends set him—not of course that she would supply them, until he had indicated that perhaps, she might." (5) Dandekar, torn between the two ambivalent attitudes, conceded reverence but the difference was a fine point as due to a symbol and its actuality. More disturbing to him is the fact that Sarojini is bound up in socio-cultural beliefs that imply reposing faith in a Swamy for her cure. When he meets her cousin Rajam he cries out: "what makes you so gullible . . . as to believe these hearsay stories, these cures that have happened always to someone else." (114) That Rajam herself was cured by the Swamy comes as a shock to him. Yet he will brook no chance and would prefer Sarojini to be chemically treated. As Sarojini says: "I do not expect you to understand—you with your western notions, your superior talk of ignorance and superstition when all it means is that you don't know what lies beyond reason and you prefer not to find out." For a while Dandekar feels nettled but he lapses into his earlier positivism which he shares with his colleagues daily. The influence of the western culture is keenly felt in the office. There is Joseph who believed in "free love and was even said to practise it." Ghose the senior officer, eager to catch up with the west, dismisses the Swamy as an impostor living in apparent poverty to hide his murky dealings.

But there is also Sastri who like Dandeker believed that Indian society rested on the morals of its women. Sastri saw films of Indian classical stories and held "the benign belief that wives were faithful, virtuous creatures prepared like their sisters to follow their husbands barefoot into the jungle." (23)

Dandeker's life had been contented, peaceful, his home quiet, and Sarojini served him a hot meal. But with her frequent absences from home he was forced to have a cold meal. He had "never cooked a meal, never fried a chilly or a potato. Men never did, unless they were cooks and even cooks wouldn't cook in their own homes." (139) Dandeker is himself at conflict with his eastern and western notions. His eldest daughter Lakshmi, without her mother's surveillance at home, frequents the milk bar which goes against the culture and social beliefs that are entrenched in Dandekar. His middle-class living goes hand in hand with his middle-class predicament rooted in traditional social patterns and culture, yet willing it away.

The socio-cultural economic conflicts of the East and the West are more directly manifest in Markandaya's fourth novel *Possession*. Lady Caroline Bell who represents that West is "magnolia white . . . in a company that was divided between brown and brick red." (7) She was rich and also divorced. It was the Indian prince Jumbo, called so, "not because of his size, but because it was the custom for people of his class to be given nicknames . . . because of the English upper-class predilection for them" (9) who brought together Caroline the daughter of his one-time English Resident and the young liberated Indian writer Anasuya. Together they make their way to an Indian village, which "isn't like an English one," in a bizarre search for country liquor. Amidst the grinding poverty of the village, Caroline stumbles upon the goat-herd Valmiki who paints amateurishly but attracts her attention. Her materialistic instincts lead her to barter for him, and she is successful in taking him away. Valmiki's life with his family, as he later reminisces, had not been a very happy one. After his childhood not providing himself a good farm hand, he was entrusted only with the goats and given the least care and love. He grew up with other "rejects" of society like the mad woman and the cripple in the wilderness outside the village, under the love and care of the Swamy to whom he becomes inalienably-attached. He takes the Swamy's blessings before he leaves the village. But after the initial excitement of travelling to England, Valmiki seems to find no source of inspiration for his art. Anasuya the writer who tells us Valmiki's story notes the gradual metamorphosis which he undergoes while being indoctrinated into English living and culture. The incongruities worked "quite impartially whether by making a monkey out of Caroline with her gloves and her art enthusiasms in the artless backwoods of a tropical country or by laying the same bizarre wand on Valmiki hatted and suited on his way to the Savoy or listening with me to Bach." (85-86) But the assimilation of the foreign culture was not always a dismal result for it could rise "beyond grotesquerie to become unique and splendid, like the British in India, like Caroline overcoming the worst of foreign temperament and terrain." (85-86) Valmiki too gradually overcomes his Indian conditioning to adjust to England so that unlike Anasuya who was only a bird of passage he did not perhaps feel that "sudden tug of the land" when experiencing "the sheer opulence of never feeling cold" in England's midsummer.

Valmiki grows up in Caroline's house tended by the Indian Tamil cook and the English housekeeper Mrs. Peabody. The Indian and the English attitudes towards work are also conflicting. In Mrs. Peabody's opinion the Indian cook didn't "know where to start, never having the habit of work" whereas she could see nothing dirty and therefore scrubbed and polished the floor till it shone. Unlike the English who were individualistic and self-reliant the Indians were always part of a group so that as Mrs. Peabody observes of Valmiki that he was so only because he never had much to do with looking after himself; unlike those in her own family. Mrs. Peabody had ventured to invite the Indian cook home to Sunday dinner and considered it a big privilege extended to a foreigner whom one could never trust. His refusal she took for an insult to herself whom she deemed superior. The servant in India is a class by itself. Anasuya describes his role as he "padded unobtrusively . . . all without a second glance at me, in the tradition that his caste and mine both acquiesced in." (95) Even if the servant was a man, it was his duty in life to perform any service for his mistress and she as mistress was expected never to swerve from her attitude.

Valmiki graduates in anglicization; he kisses Anasuya on the cheek when earlier he had compared her to his sister and brought her "parijata" flowers. He resorts to painting that is no longer inspired by spiritualism but by the western aestheticism of physical beauty. Although he gives up the finer points in his culture he continues to dwell on his habit of cracking his knuckles. This detour into a foreign culture does not contain him long though and he is pulled back. The Swamy's visit to England, at the invitation of his English disciples, revitalizes the cords of culture. On a visit to India, Anasuya had seen how the Swamy was besieged by these foreign women mostly and she sought a "public audience in the natural, shameless, uninhibited manner of India" and despite her own westernisms felt no need for "the western yen for privacy, the castle to contain oneself." (97)

Caroline too cannot pull herself away completely from her social superiority and continues making fun of the Indian sense of punctuality, "the oriental's wish to finger every pie," to never go "whole-hog—singe its bristles but never do it in."

The economic disparities of the East and the West underlie Caroline's patronage of Valmiki's art. In his own home there is no need for art on an empty stomach and is considered wasteful occupation. Caroline's security on the other hand encourages her to adopt the artist boy for ends of her own. The Indian village is full of the poor, even the little child who directed Caroline hopes for a "baksheesh" from Caroline who is synonymous with English wealth and ruler. Yet the sovereigns that Caroline sends Valmiki's mother as a poor compensation for Valmiki are not used by her but kept as contingency for the boy when he marries. She herself lies dying in her meagre surroundings and poor care without even basic comforts. Anasuya is plagued by the anomalous situation and quizzes at the irony of what to leave with such a person, "wireless, television, ovaltine, flowers . . . that were the established rights of the bedridden British?" (169)

A Handful of Rice portrays the socio-cultural economic clash more vividly than the previous novels. Ravi has left his home in the village to seek a better existence in the city and is torn between both values and undergoes a crisis in character. Once again Markandaya gives a graphic description of an Indian village where its people "lived between bouts of genteel and acute proverty—the kind in which the weakest went to the wall, the old ones and the babies dying of tuberculosis, dysentery, the 'falling fever,' 'recurrent fever' and any other names for what was basically, simply nothing but starvation." (12) Ravi like his brothers is given some learning by a father who believes that "better things than were due to a man who could read and write, better things than working with his hands for a pittance, things for instance like working in a government office for one hundred rupees per mensem and a pension when he retired." (39) But in the city there was no job for them between coolie and clerk so that it was like a jungle of riff-raffs hanging around all day doing nothing. And the father who had craved to have sons who would help him work in the fields is left to tend it himself. He must mortgage portions of it to meet any contingency as he does before making a trip to the city to finalize Ravi's marriage.

In the city, Ravi discovers that life for the poor is no different. Economically they are as deprived, toiling hard for meagre wages; exploited by the rich towns people. The English Memsahibs and the Indian ones haggled over prices. Apu, the old tailor, into whose house Ravi had forced himself one night in a state of drunkenness when chased by the police, treats his clients as little gods. He works hard to please them, bribes their watchman to be allowed into those big houses with marble floors and cool interiors; is made to use the backstairs like sweepers but he does not complain. Neither does his daughter Nalini, whom Ravi loves and marries. She believes that people of their kind cannot hope to be so rich. But Ravi rebels against such economic disparity. He knows that the rich belong to the same class the world over: "the sameness makes them stick together." It was economic stability that made them use that commanding tone. It was their money that brought them the power to do the pushing around. The Memsahib who had a lot of clothes stitched in India because "things were so cheap here . . . knew she would never be able to afford so many clothes once she left India." She had no sympathy for the workman who made this possible. On Apu's death when Ravi takes over his work and explains the delay in the delivery, she is not prepared to accept his reasons for the delay. Ravi reflects on her callousness: "Did this woman realise how they lived? The duties and ceremonies that fell upon the head of the house? In her community," he wondered, "did they simply carry straight on after a death as if nothing happened?" (184) He felt convinced that "nothing lays down they should always have the best and trample over us and do us down and we should always come off worst." (75) The town was associated with such evils that were considered a western impact.

Socially and culturally the tailor Apu has not been changed by the town. He had hoped for a son like any farmer in the village to help him with his trade. His home in the city is full of relatives who do no work and live off him. Apu does not complain and never thinks of "booting out" any relative. But to the rebel Ravi, in his degenerated phase when all that matters is money, these relatives are parasites and he shows them the door. He soon realizes the advantage of the old system but only after much harm is done. In the initial stages Ravi had seen some of the advantages in the system when he began to fall in love with Apu's young daughter Nalini. Marriages in India are not founded on love, as Jayamma's showed. She was much younger than Apu and did not love him. But in his illness she nursed him "devotedly as a wife should out of a strong sense of duty." In the village "young men came to know young girls within the approving carefully conducted circle of mutual friends and family relationships." A strict watch was kept on the girls unlike the shameless ways of Europeans and Americans. Women had information on girls who came of age and boys looking for brides went back and forth to arrange marriages. The living together of all the members had advantages; you were never left stranded. Ravi, when he forsakes this, finds himself alone, desperate, unhappy, "a fish out of water." He has an incestuous relationship with his mother-in-law, beats his wife Nalini whom he had loved dearly. But "who cares what goes on between four walls? It's the public scandal that breaks one in two?" The author comments on the sham and hypocrisy of social values. Once Ravi's intrinsic innocence is lost he becomes one of the jungle, that is, the city, at whose feet all the evils have been dumped.

In *The Coffer Dams,* the conflict is accentuated in real encounters between the Indian and English engineers. The English engineers come to India with memories of the colonial past. "We like keeping ourselves to ourselves," said Jackson. They proceed to build their little Englands "in the orderly scene . . . the trim square plots of emerging garden, the gravelled paths, the white washed boulders that demarcate and uphold private property rights." (11) They took precautions against the dangers of drinking polluted water and living in "tiger country." Fenced in securely, they believed no good came out of associating with the Indians and believed in sticking together. The Indians on their part kept away from the English because of their new found independence and also because they were convinced of their culture being superior to the others. There were few occasions for them to meet socially and when the neutral Englishman associated with the Indians like Helen and Lefevre did, the others ranged against them. The Rawlings were appalled to see Lefevre bring Gopal Rao as a companion to their dinner. "Look what the lad's brought in," cried Millie Rawlings and though her husband asked her not to make a scene about it he discreetly refused to shake hands with Gopal Rao resorting to a "namaste" instead, even while shaking hands with his own kinsmen.

Even though Clinton was the head of the operations he had no idea where his Indian labourers came from or went into, trailing mountain paths into the jungle, or from which they came in "one dark wave of humanity" after another. And the civilized Indians and English both looked down upon the tribals which only emphasized that each was equally guilty of discrimination. Helen was different. She believed in them as being human beings and overcame the burden of getting beyond the skin.

The English who took pride in being well-advanced in technical know-how doubted whether the Indians would ever be able to acquire what was "in the bone" of the Englishman. This gave them power over the Indians and fuelled their superiority complex. It was further intensified by their economic solidity. They believed themselves to be the real sahibs and "Mems" who shopped in the big city emporia. But they were unwittingly "flattered and mulcted" by the Indian shopkeepers who really held them in contempt. They left behind the money cult which the tribal chief said would really be "a peace full of mourning" for it would leave the tribals "pining for trash."

The power of the English and their money won them the devoted services of Indian servants. Some like Das, in contrast to their English masters, lived huddled in blankets and rugs in their icy godowns. But it did not deter them from their service in life which was to provide comfort to their master doing things they believed were in fact a wife's duty to do, like pummelling the calves to loosen knots. The English wife was not subservient and would only go as far as the neck muscles. There was a more equal standing between the English men and women. Lefevre could talk freely with two young English girls which Gopal Rao was shy to do; so "unused to chatting with girls," he would not have known where to begin.

In *The Nowhere Man,* the cultural ties of the East cannot be sundered easily by the expatriate Srinivas and his wife Vasantha, nor social habits shed easily. When Vasantha receives a telegram from her son about his marriage to an English girl, she is too shocked to return inside till an English neighbour, quite unused to open show of emotion, leads her in. "The way these Indians went to pieces. Different from one's own kind who would close the door and pull down the blind decently, not stand about letting the whole world see," (31-32) reflects the English lady. Vasantha's son Laxman, bred in England, is equally embarrassed by his mother's Indianness in dress and speech and he feels she sticks out "like a sore thumb." When a son is born to him, he specifically asks his parents not to visit them as the spare bedroom had been taken up by his wife's parents. Vasantha is surprised that the lack of another room should so deter him when she was prepared to sleep in the corridor or kitchen only to be able to see her grandchild. But Srinivas reminds her that "they don't do things like that in this country." Laxman, they feel, has "moved too far away from us," for he seems disinclined to help with hospital bills and the care his mother needs in her state of tuberculosis. He considers the National Health quite sufficient for her. When Vasantha dies, Srinivas is even lonelier till an English lady Mrs. Pickering in simple friendliness seems to notice his distraught condition. She was not more communicative because "the English do not like their reserve invaded" yet Srinivas recognized her familiar figure again and "would have launched himself upon her with glad cries, this being the first reaction of his blood, but England intervened. England with its unvoiced interdictions which had laid halter and curb on him, cooling the riper manifestations of emotions." (50) Mrs. Pickering despite her friendliness was English and did not like people to pry and "force themselves upon you for their benefit and pretend it's for yours."

When Mrs. Pickering moves in to share Srinivas's house she works hard at keeping the house clean, "squalor is offensive to the English." But Srinivas is also fastidious about "personal cleanliness, those finicky habits he had carried with him from India and clung to despite the different equipment in England." (61) As he confesses to Mrs. Pickering, "when one leaves one's country how much is chopped off and left behind too. The inconsiderable which one does not even think of at the time, which are in fact important." (70) He cannot refrain from smiling at neighbours even though they did not care for this open show of feeling. The Indians were instinctive, emotional whereas the English were rational and materialistic. Mrs. Pickering admits that to be allowed to live in peace in England, "affluence is the keynote, the key."

Two Virgins sums up the hackneyed theme of traditional Indian life as against the modern western outlook with Aunt Alamelu at one end and Appa at the other. Every opportunity afforded by such a theme is exploited. The author castigates an amorphous entity called society and western materialism associated with cities.

The story of the two virgins Lalitha and Saroja is a tedious description of village life that an "Indian writer living permanently abroad cannot always be trusted to write knowingly about."[4] Markandaya's being "too long in the West" has drawn forth a vituperative attack on the influence of the West that has ruined Indian traditional society and the social evils of this tradition that impeded its progress. The conflict of socio-cultural and economic values of the East and the West has in a sense been the rape of an ancient civilization.

The two virgins live with Appa, Amma and the widowed Aunt Alamelu who had no husband and therefore no status. To Appa the liberated Westerner, the joint family is an anachronism. Aunt Alamelu feels it is directed against her and says: "just tell me to go and I will, I know I have outlived my usefulness. . . . I am only a widow, less than the dust so do not torment yourself about my fate." (20) Orphans and those without fathers like Saroja's confidant Chingleput, the sweetmeat-maker, was also one of society's destitutes. Society's rejection of such people is borne out in the monkey incident when Chingleput tells Saroja: "it ought to have been left to die as its mother intended when she abandoned it, because the tribe would never accept a cripple." (18) There were other ways in which the Indian society was split. The differences in caste kept Mr. Gupta the film-maker and Lalitha the aspiring actress on different scales: "the truth was that although both were Hindus, which was the important thing, their levels were different . . . unequal society." (179) Chingleput of course was "beyond the pole" and the pariahs were the worst of all. It was their job to keep things clean they were used to handling filth and Amma disapproved that now-a-days they were getting above themselves. Appa the freedom fighter, liberated in his outlook, reminds her of Gandhi's preaching that all were children of God which is totally unacceptable to Amma who believes "it is their Karma their fate" to have been born into that caste.

Marriages could only take place between people of the same caste in India. Even then it was important that "the star you were born under had to be in harmony with your husband's. If they were inimical the marriage was doomed . . . you couldn't have been allowed to marry in the first place." (205)

Appa's ideas are modern and occasionally smack of the permissiveness of contemporary Western society. But he is forced to fall in line with society's code when he decides with Amma that their daughter's illegitimate child be aborted. Lalitha is considered not so much a breaker of moral rules as that of social, traditional rules.

Miss Mendoza and the film-maker Mr. Gupta are considered pernicious Western influences. Amma and Aunt Alamelu vehemently denounce her high-heeled shoes and his cream silk suits. Miss Mendoza's style of living is contemptuously viewed. She was a Christian and in the opinion of the two Hindu ladies "spitting and hawking were the unclean habits of the Christians who did not mind about spittle, thought nothing of using the same drinking cups." (189) The Europeans ate a lot, they believed, and would stop at nothing so that Amma and Aunt Alamelu sniffed disparagingly at the jellies Miss Mendoza made which the other two believed were hoofs and horns boiled. Appa however approved of the "urbane intercourse between men and women as a mark of civilization." Aunt Alamelu did not approve of this "simpering with youngmen and flaunting themselves. There was no propriety in it and totally contrary to the code of our Hindu decorum which has safeguarded the virtues of our youth for a thousand years."

On the economic front, western society subordinated everything to the motive of bigger profits. During the famine in the days of the Raj Appa felt they considered themselves "too superior to go round and see how the poor people were faring." India had been reduced to beggary because English goods had been thrust on her and consequently her own handicrafts dwindled. In Amma's view the English doctors with their advanced knowledge of science "think they are gods, they have no religion, no ethic or scruple to restrain them" and the Indian doctors were influenced by them. But most of India was so poor that many "sat in a long row and held out their begging bowls" near temples whereas those who were too respectable to beg but very poor queued for a free meal the priests handed out once daily. Their poverty and under-nourishment brought about health hazards. The blacksmith who worked hard coughed "bits of his lungs." They are naturally worried then that the introduction of machines would kill them further, as Chingelput dreads, because it would make a cut into his sale of sweets.

The Golden Honeycomb probes once more the problems of socio-cultural economic adjustments between the East and the West. Humanity is all one but gets split up by externals into different water-tight compartments and that can be diffused only with love and understanding.

The Englishman in India in this novel is of that class which "sincerely believed that India could do no better than submit to the British presence." Their presumed superiority kept them aloof and they were even disdainful of the Indian in his social habits and scorned their culture which seemed to them barbaric. The Indians themselves were stratified according to the caste into which one was born. Each caste was designated its own work. The Brahmins were of the highest order, men of learning and therefore priests and Prime Ministers like the Dewan in this novel. The Kshatriyas were second in that social hierarchy. Being of the warrior class they were the rulers but even the ruler had to bend to touch the Brahmin's feet. So interwoven was this social stratification that in the novel under study, the British despite their power could not shatter the caste-mould when appointing a new ruler of Devapur. They had at first selected one of the Vaishya caste but this was a caste of traders and the English, ironically traders themselves, were not allowed to tamper with the accepted social pattern.

Markandaya highlights the ironies of these man-made barriers. The Brahmin Dewan and the English Resident were both professionally similar, learned in their ways, punctilious in their dress, fastidious in cleanliness. Yet each viewed the other with distrust and as being a contaminating influence. The Brahmin with his strict code of purity and cleanliness changed and bathed "after the hurly-burly of audience to rid himself of the scent of natives and feringhi." (6) To him every person other than a Brahmin was polluted and the foreigner more so because he "enjoyed the consumption of animal carcasses." He would care to keep a reasonable distance between himself and the British Agent. The latter was no different. He resorted to smoking cigarettes to rid his nostrils of the whiff of curry. No Brahmin household would eat food cooked by any other than the Brahmin cook and he got the same respect. But these cooks would never enter any regimental cook-house which had to keep cooks of the lowest and fourth level of the Indian caste, who were not supposed to be defiled by anybody or anything however low and dirty being of that same category. The foreigner in India was considered a "mllechha" by the Indian. The foreigner too looked down upon the Indian.

The Brahmin Minister did not enter the birth chamber at the birth of the Prince because it was "unclean" and would do so only after purification. The Dewan's wife Vatsala did not want the Resident to defile her household by crossing its threshold. When the Resident did so, he had to walk in his stockinged feet. After he had drunk from a silver goblet Vatsala had it melted down to purify it.

The Resident too found the drink "revolting" and the scent of the tuberoses in Vatsala's hair, the rose water sprinkled on him by the children proved deterrent to a return invitation to the Dewan and his wife. The Resident knew these things would prove totally unacceptable to his wife. He reflects that "but for the women they might have been friends," even though their friendship might not attain great heights.

Indian rituals and ceremonies are dealt with extravagantly, to juxtapose them with the Englishman's lack of appreciation or understanding of them. The wedding of Bawajiraj II at nineteen with revelry and rejoicing and colour "wearies the Agent, whose constitution wilts before these scenes of unremitting enthusiasm." (22-23) Yet at the Durbar in Delhi the Englishmen put up a spectacular show of pomp, grandeur and brass bands. The Dowager Maharani's widowhood is given a detailed description to familiarize an audience ignorant of it. Bawajiraj II's flirtations with Mohini, her being pregnant with his child are viewed with a moral disgust by the British. They cannot trust the Indians and when this illegitimate boy Rabi grows up to love the Resident's daughter Sophie, she cannot help recalling the warning that he had been born on the wrong side of the sheet.

Bawajiraj's wife Shanta Devi lives a life apart from her husband reconciled to the belief that "she must submit to men in general and to her husband in particular." The wife did not take her husband's name as Vatsala did not and even Rukmani in *Nectar in a Sieve* did not.

Bawajiraj II as a ruler is contrasted with the British Resident. Despite his Western training, Bawajiraj likes flash and colours bright and bold. The Resident on the other hand has planned his drawing room and private suite "to pacify body and spirit to anticipate and fulfil the wants of the human frame and the hankering of the soul in exile." (99) There is none of the noise and confusion that prevails outside these quarters. Bawajiraj preferred however the British verbal understatement pared to the reality both perceived and invisible, of a quite stunning order of magnificence. But there were other traits in him that were Indian. During the famine, Lady

Copeland distributed tea and rice to orderly queues of the starving. But Bawajiraj flung generous handfuls of coins to the poor who actively and enthusiastically supported him despite everything, so was their conditioning.

The English who seemed so commanding and imperious in their roles in India were in their own country agreeable and charming people. Unfortunately there was a chasm that yawned between them and the natives in India so that they constantly viewed the other with hate, distrust and suspicion.

III

Ruth Prawer Jhabvala by virtue of her marriage to an Indian has taken a keen interest in Indian life. She has gained an intimate understanding of the ideas, ideals and various lifestyles of the Indians. She highlights, to comic proportions, the incongruous blending of the Eastern and the Western modes of life.

In *To Whom She Will,* Amrita has been brought up in an anglicized way in India. Her grandfather, Pandit Ram Bahadur Saxena, is an anglophile, well-travelled over the continent with a home stocked with mementos from his travels. He lives and speaks English but his wife now dead had been "small and gentle and old even in middle age, with her hands folded and the sari covering her head." (11) Amrita in her pseudo-Westernism runs after romance and the idea of love. But the man she fancies herself in love with, Hari Sahni—a colleague at the All India Radio—is far removed in his ways and lifestyle: "He was simple and unspoilt, and his ways the traditional, truly Indian ways which had been lost in her family." (30) Each loved the other or thought so, for such conflicting ways. Hari Sahni aimed at cultivating Amrita's westernisms while she tried hard to give up her western ways and submit herself wholly to Hari Sahni in the traditional way. Ironically they are married to partners arranged for them. Hari Sahni "was used to having all his relations at the back of him, and existence without that support and security seemed almost impossible to him." (131) Even while plans to elope with Amrita appeal to his romantic side, he cannot find the going easy and leaves his mother and sister to arrange for his marriage. His sister Prema had been intimidated by Amrita's forward ways and the opulence of Amrita's mother, Radha. Prema therefore decides to get Hari married soon to the demure Sushila Anand who is "one of us." Hari's mother makes sure to make known to Mrs. Anand that her son had been offered huge dowries but it was not the money only but the girl that they were interested in. Hari surprisingly is not gnawed by any guilt-complexes and readily acquiesces to the marriage. He feels elated because being on "the boy's side," they "had no responsibilities, they could feast, enjoy themselves and send for their relations all at the expense of the bride's family." (199)

Radha was just as frantic to find a match for Amrita who was well-educated abroad and had a secure government job of high position. Like her sister Tarla, she believed in the liberation of women, the Hindu Code Bill "but it is quite different when one thinks of one's own daughter." (127)

The socio-cultural conflict is innate in all such Indians themselves and the economic conflict is often the deciding factor, Jhabvala seems to suggest. In *The Nature of Passion* the traditional undivided Hindu family of Lala Narayan Dass Verma—Lalaji—is threatened by the "westernized" attitudes of his daughter Nimmi and son Chandra and Viddi. At eighteen, Nimmi rebels against the narrowness of the life of the women's quarters and the system of arranged marriages with dowry. She longs for a gay, emancipated life and to break away from the stifling orthodoxy of the women of her family. She frequents the club and even dates a Parsi playboy, Pheroze Batliwala. Jhabvala underlines Nimmi's snobbishness, her posturing before Rajan as an emancipated woman which shows up for what it is. The symbol of emancipation for Nimmi is to have her hair cut short—an act daring enough in the suffocating atmosphere of her orthodox family life.

Lala's cleverest son Chandra has his education abroad and is married to an intellectual snob Kanta who detests everything about Lalaji family, their coarseness, their old-fashioned ways, their rigid orthodoxy, their corruptness, everything indeed except their money. Chandra with tragic finality is cut off from his family because it is only he who can extricate his father from the bribery case in which he is involved. To Kanta only his promotion is of any consequence and she hosts dinner parties to promote him. Nimmi admires her "liberated" sister-in-law and is introduced to the people who come to one such party. She "instinctively greeted the visitors with her palms joined together in Indian style and only realised how unsuitable this was when the other Indians shook hands with her and tolerantly smiled." Kanta and Nimmi considered their every gesture important in this new sophisticated world, which they hoped would help redeem their old-fashioned life.

Viddi the youngest son is a disenchanted, disaffected bohemian, idling his time in a cafe with pseudo-artists. Viddi prides himself on his good luck in falling in with these gentlemen so utterly removed, he feels, from sordid bourgeois money-making. He fails to see however that they have befriended him only to get as much money as possible out of him. Far from sharing his contempt for money they worship it more avidly than Lalaji.

Lalaji is a corrupt but benevolent emperor of the capital whose life is devoted to providing for the welfare of a large united family, at any cost. His eldest son Om, is like Lalaji, a hungry capitalist. Lalaji knows he must make and preserve a fortune by expanding his business empire for his family. The pursuit gets Lalaji mixed-up in a great corruption-scandal in which he badly needs the cooperation of Dev Rai, Om's father-in-law and a rival millionaire whose family is despised and resented by Lalaji. Om is starkly different from Chandra and Viddi, orthodox and ruthless in business. He attends parties not in clubs but where young prostitutes provide entertainment.

Lalaji instinctively clings to the old orthodox Hindu way, its rituals and customs. His shrewdness and his money save Viddi and Nimmi from leaving him and the family and probably ruining themselves. Like that of Amrita of the first novel, Nimmi's marriage is arranged but the husband chosen for her is none other than her new friend Kuku who is of her own religion and community. Viddi too rejoins the family and the business.

In *Esmond in India*, there is a more direct clash between the Englishman Esmond and his Indian wife Gulab, as also between the Westernized rich materialistic family of Har Dayal and the idealism of Ram Nath.

Esmond scrapes a living in India by giving private lessons in Hindi, Indian history and literature to English memsahibs, tourists and rich Indian sophisticates. He is not as rich as Lakshmi, Ram Nath's wife, suspects all Englishmen to be; there is no convincing reason as to why he married Gulab, Uma's daughter and Ram Nath's niece. The marriage deteriorates rapidly after the birth of a son Ravi, adored and spoilt by his mother Gulab and her mother Uma. Esmond is probably at the stage where he finds "everything Indian abominable."[5] The marriage becomes a battlefield with Esmond trying to make Gulab bring Ravi up in the European way, keeping him from sweet foods and not spoiling him with caresses. But Gulab reverts to Indian ways when Esmond is not there, lavishing sweet and sentimental love on the child, eating rich spicy Indian food, lying on the floor and using all the strong scents that Esmond finds stifling. Her mother Uma begs her to leave Esmond and to come home. Even her idealistic uncle Ram Nath reasons: "He is a very different person from you and he does not understand you and the way you live and think, the way we all live and think. I think he should not be in this country at all, because he in no way belongs here." (164) Esmond is cruel with Gulab, savagely sarcastic, pinching and slapping her but Gulab meekly surrenders, accepting the traditional role of the Indian wife to whom the husband is a god. She resists leaving Esmond till the end of the novel, disgusted and furious only after a servant tries to rape her during one of Esmond's protracted absences. She then blames Esmond for the attack and leaves him for good with her son Ravi.

Disgusted with Gulab's passivity and love for Indian oils and strong scents, food and speech, Esmond finds consolation in Betty. She was "so light, modern and airy. Being with her was almost as good as being in England—which was the one place where he wanted most passionately to be." (49) In India, he felt he could only have been happily married into a rich and influential family with an elegant drawing room like the one he had had tea in, with Madhuri, Har Dayal's wife, and her daughter-in-law Indira. Ironically he did have occasion to flirt with Shakuntala, Har Dayal's bright, young, would-be bohemian daughter, a romantic straight out of college. Shakuntala despises her mother's and Indira's materialism and dotes on her father Har Dayal whom she does not see for the scheming politician that he is but finds him a man of culture, reciting the Sanskrit poems at parties. She is led into her father's sophisticated circle of expatriates and rich Indians and she meets and falls romantically in love with the flamboyant Esmond. In a bid to be emancipated, she even accompanies a group of English ladies to Agra with Esmond as guide. She blames Gulab for being "slow and stupid" and unfit for the company of European ladies. Esmond was not wrong in leaving her behind. She competes with the Billimoria sisters at being more westernized and finds "no harm in men and women being friends. In Europe everybody is like that." (148) She admires the graceful ease, relaxed manner and the fairness of Esmond and Betty and finds herself heavy, dark and dull by contrast. Yet even she is revolted by the sight of their drinking from the same bottle. Flattered by Esmond's advances she allows herself to be seduced by him in her hotel room, without much difficulty. After that, Shakuntala finds herself wholly committed to him. All she wanted to do was to worship him and serve and adore him, to be his slave. To Esmond it was "nothing, just a poke in the eye" because he had been annoyed with Betty. But to Shakuntala, "it was the beginning and the end of the world." To Esmond a wife was meant to be "a friend and companion, not my slave." Gulab knowing none of this thought kindly of Shakuntala and even hoped that "she would marry a charming young man from her own community whom her parents would choose for her."

Despite Shakuntala's idealism she does not consider marrying Narayan, Ram Nath's doctor-son who works among the poor tribals. It is what her mother also thinks for her. Ram Nath's economic conditions deter Har Dayal from contemplating a marriage alliance with the other's family. Both families share the common practices of an Indian joint family in which the family sits together to decide vital issues like marriage alliances. Jhabvala makes note in her essay "Myself in India" that in India "it is the family or clan members who gather together and enjoy each other's company."[6]

The Householder is centred on the married life of Prem and his young wife Indu. The tale is told with gentle mocking irony. Prem is not a good degree-holder and is lucky to have got a job. He teaches in a private college owned by the pompous Mr. Khanna and his even more odious wife who do not pay their staff well but thrive on the profits that the college fetches. They also treat their staff with scant respect. They are almost Dickensian in their comic awfulness. To Prem his role of householder is seriously affected by his meagre resources. To make matters worse Prem's landlord Mr. Seigal threatens to raise the rent. Prem is economically deprived in the traditional role of being a householder.

Prem is acutely conscious of his dignity as a "Professor" and feels uncertainty and shame in his desire for his wife's body. He constantly recalls the fact that his father had been a college principal. Prem's and Indu's marriage has been an arranged one. He scarcely knows his wife Indu and what he knows he dislikes and despises. Prem's mother comes to live with them. Prem's wife Indu wants her to go away. Prem is too tied to his mother's apron-strings to want to break away. Temporarily he is restored to his bachelorhood and feels a trifle happier but soon he becomes aware of his growing love for Indu for whom he buys that symbolic piece of pink satin. But his mother's possessiveness fills him with remorse so that he gives that piece to her to cheer her up. When Indu returns, the young couple are embarrassed in their love-making with Prem's mother's presence in the house. Prem plans to send her to his sister and is so relieved when she does go that he does not wait to see the train go as he hurries to his wife Indu.

In *Get Ready for Battle,* Gulzari Lal is a rich Punjabi business man who has largely adopted a western manner of life though "he still liked to sit on the floor and eat his food from little bowls with his fingers." (26) He adhered to the breakfast of his youth, of fried puris and lentils and pickles. He is a shrewd businessman ever-concerned with improving his business deals. He decides to buy the land at Bundi Busti for his economic gains unaffected by the slum-dwellers who would be ousted. In the same category are the snobbish and hypocritical do-gooders like Mrs. Bhatnagar who think nothing of the slum-dwellers in their euphemistic bid to do social service. Gulzarilal is brought into direct conflict with his wife Sarla Devi.

Sarla Devi is a Gandhian idealist concerned only with thwarting her husband's plans to evict the slum-dwellers from Bundi Busti. She lives away from him and his wealth. To her it is of little concern that Gulzari Lal should divorce her. His mistress, the widow Kusum Mehra, who stands to gain, coaxes Gulzari Lal time and again to legitimatize their relationship. Kusum Mehra is servile in her care for the rich Gulzari Lal and does her best to woo his son Vishnu and Sarla Devi's brother Brij Mohan to her side. Sarla Devi is fond of Vishnu but his wife does not think kindly of her because she has left her rightful home. Sarla Devi quite unconventionally seeks an apology from her son's wife for visiting her. Vishnu's westernized friends also annoy his wife to a degree of causing an estrangement between them. These young sophisticates dance to western music at Toto Saxena's party, drink alcohol, flirt and talk politics with cursory knowledge culled from *Time* and *Femina*. Their intellectualism is not only hollow but cruelly divorced from the real India of Bundi Bustis so that Jhabvala hints these young sophisticates will turn into future Mrs. Bhatnagars. Ironically, while they try to control the birth rate the masses blithely buy fertility charms from pedlars. More pathetic is Brij Mohan who though highly-educated and westernized is dragged into poverty by his laziness and addiction to whisky and women. Dissipation and the calamity of the partition of India and Pakistan had reduced Brij Mohan to a caricature of his old self so that he believes that "when my compensation comes I shall be a different man. Then people will treat me again with the respect which is due to me." (52)

Like Sarla Devi, Gautam is also crying out for change in age-old conventions without really submitting to an alien culture. Symbolically he does not approve of western furniture for an Indian society, just as he does not approve of the girl Sumi being married to someone she has never seen. If her brother-in-law asserts that her parents choose with love and care Gautam cries out: "Hasn't she a mind and heart of her own to choose with." Gautam is in a hurry to change old customs and ways, just as Sarla Devi wants to change economic imbalances.

A Backward Place is the reaction of westernized Indians and expatriates to India. Here, as in *Esmond in India,* Indians and expatriates are brought into direct confrontation. The expatriate Europeans or westerners pass through three levels or stages in India, according to Jhabvala. They are either loving everything Indian or finding "everything Indian not so marvellous; third state, everything Indian abominable."[7] The problems of expatriates in their various stages of assimilation and negation of India are all a part of the socio-cultural economic conflict that they suffer.

First of all let us look at Judy who is married to an Indian actor generally out of work. Judy has to a considerable extent become Indian, adopted Indian attitudes, and has to the extent possible assumed an Indian personality. According to Jhabvala, Judy may be at peace by giving in and wearing a sari, becoming meek and accepting. But she is a product of a lonely and tragic English middle-class family and finds the friendly promiscuous and comforting disorder of the joint family enjoyable. At the same time she has also proved her European defiance and gone to work becoming ironically the bread-winner of her family. She hungers for a permanent home and believes in staying secure where she is, instead of going to Bombay with the reckless Bal where they know no one and have no place to stay.

Clarissa is a young English eccentric, in love with India of the sages and gurus. Her dream-India has little relevance to the real India typified by the beggars who pluck at her sari, make fun of her and arouse momentary anger in her. She lives in squalor and has constant trouble with her successive landlords. In spite of her wretchedness she cannot leave India. She hungers for the permanence of a home and familial love. She is therefore wavering between the first and second stages of living in India.

Etta, the middle-aged Hungarian blonde is at the final stage which rejects all things Indian. She had come to India as the wife of an Indian student but the marriage had ended in divorce after which she had gone through a succession of husbands and lovers only to find herself desperately alone in an India which she hates. She is conscious of the bad smells, the ketchup stains on the table cloth, and is no longer fascinated by India. India to her is "the backward place" which she longs to leave like Esmond in *Esmond in India*. Etta is drawn to an unreal Europe of her nostalgic memories and hits out at Judy's ludicrous and shameful submission to an unworthy husband. Like Esmond, Etta is still on the search for a rich Indian patron who can keep her in luxury with trips to Europe at frequent intervals. She refuses to adapt and is on occasions even crushed by environment.

Dr. Hochstadt and his wife are temporary visitors to India, sympathetic to everything Indian, condoning the faults and foibles of "the backward place" in a slightly patronizing way. Without facing the problems of expatriation, they preach the necessity for Europeans to adapt themselves to the Indian rhythm.

On the Indian side, Bal, Judy's feckless husband, is a graduate. The fact had impressed her at first but later she discovered that every other Indian was so without being any the better for it. Bal is without a job but is devoted to his pipe-dream of becoming a great actor one day. He firmly believes that playing second fiddle to the Bombay actor Kishan Kumar will provide him the break that will bring him wealth and fame. He does not feel embarrassed by his wife supporting him till he is one day insulted by the cynical Etta after which he assumes the role of the householder and urges Judy to lay off work and sets about planning to go to Bombay in search of work. Although Bal is married to an English, he feels embarrassed being kissed by her in the presence of the others in her office. "Some one will see" is his Indian reaction. Similarly he cannot get over his revulsion at the European habit of drinking from the same cup. To him "it was deeply repugnant to touch his lips to where someone else's had been."

Bal lives in a joint family, along with his brother's family and

Bhuaji. The old windowed aunt had no immediate relative but was passed from one household to another wherever she was most needed. Her needs were frugal. Sudhir was an intelligent Bengali boy who had been forced by his poverty to take up a lucrative job at the Cultural Dais. But it was only with the recommendations of a Minister from his region who knew his family that this was possible. Bal too had been mustering some influence to obtain the patronage of the Cultural Dais and even urged his foreign wife to intercede for him because of the influence she being a foreigner would have. Sudhir however is sensitive to India's problems and does not like being a lackey to Mrs. Kaul who ran the Cultural Dais. She was a fat and fickle bourgeois "do-gooder" who cared nothing for the noble abstracts of the Cultural Dais. To her "it was an opportunity for social advancement, a place where you can meet nice and interesting people and . . . also an opportunity perhaps to wangle a trip abroad." (87) Sudhir and Judy were both appalled at the way she dismissed a needy girl from her job. Mrs. Kaul herself lived in a lovely, elegant, luxurious home, apathetic to the economic problems of the Indian people at large. Her own liveried servants lived in unsanitary quarters, drowning their troubles in drink and beating their wives. She was most unconcerned about these realities. Her work at the Cultural Dais is an escape from her gilded cage where she lives neglected by her husband and children. To Mrs. Kaul the Cultural Dais is a forum for her own genteel, foreign-travelled, English-speaking friends to gather, with scholars from abroad. She cannot accept Sudhir's underfed, deprived friends as intellectuals and feels ashamed of their gorging themselves on the sandwiches and cakes. Sudhir is neither the passive dreamer like Bal, nor the hypocritical westernized Indian like Mrs. Kaul; he is deeply concerned with delivering the goods. Gregarious as all Indians are, his conscience is personified by Jaykar, a veteran of the freedom struggle, who now takes vicarious pleasure in goading the young Sudhir to return to his idealism and abandon the Dais. Sudhir's moment of truth comes when Mrs. Kaul dismisses the girl.

There are other lesser characters like the neo-rich Mr. Gupta who was the latest Indian that Etta sought. He took Etta "as his relaxation." He overdressed with too many rings and a large gold watch but she applied her western aestheticism to tone down such extravagances. He was careful however not to take her to places where they would be seen. He was conscious of his position in his family community and political standing. Like Mrs. Kaul, he is abstracted from contemporary Indian society that apes the west and cannot at the same time cut itself away from its own. They "are not conditioned to look at themselves except with the eyes of foreign experts whom they have been taught to respect."[8]

A New Dominion develops the theme of disparities that lie between the Indians and the English who visit India after her independent statehood. Raymond is a tourist who has come visiting India. Not living in India gives his observations an objectivity towards the reasons for a conflict. He is sensitive and can enjoy India aesthetically and emotionally. Others like the young girls Lee and Margaret who have come on a spiritual quest pass through Jhabvala's European cycle.

Raymond is very sensitive to human rights and is naturally appalled to see the Indians treat their servants so violently. Most of these servants are nearly children and remind him of an England ages past. His effort to educate his Indian friend Gopi on the topic is explained away on the grounds of the servant belonging to the lowest caste who would not normally find employment in a Hindu household. There are other economic disparities that divide the rich and the poor in India. While most middle-class homes, Raymond finds, are stuffed full of possessions, unaesthetic though it may be, the poor live in a rather bleak way. Eating was the main preoccupation of those who could find food while the others died of hunger. Emaciated men were forced to pedal for a pittance passengers in the back seat and Raymond was constantly embarrassed about hiring one. On the other hand the rich like Rao Saheb added more clout by involving themselves in politics where the real power now lay. When he sells off a piece of property it is to the new rich Harish Mehta, one who studied abroad and will multiply his millions through a project that will in no way benefit the poor.

Raymond finds the Indian social and cultural values quite

intriguing. His friend Gopi who is yet to establish himself is to be married shortly. He has never seen the girl, only an uncle has gone between the families and the photograph of the bride is passed through the members of the family. A marriage in India, he discovers, is not merely between the two people but involves the two families who meet to ascertain that there are no differences between them. After thc alliance there will be numerous occasions for them to come together to share joys and sorrows.

The Indians are generally gregarious and curious to know intimate details. Raymond found this resentful habit in Gopi. He was equally shocked to note that the English in India speak in a commanding tone and look down condescendingly on anyone who didn't belong to their ilk. Their wives were just as supercilious as they had once been, meeting only the very select class of Indians at dinner-parties. Some had bcen moved to see India's poverty and had tried their hand at organized charity, only to give it up blaming it on the corruption that was rampant. And so they lived in their own little Englands, peaceably amongst themselves. Even the missionary Miss Charlotte who had lived in India for thirty years lived a life secluded in its ways from the general Indian pattern. But now that work in India was over, she wished to return home.

Lee and Margaret, the two English girls who are drawn to India by its promises of spiritual peace, do try hard to adopt Indian ways. Lee travels in the overcrowded buses full of the smell of India's poor; they even live in a primitive way at the *ashram* and try to merge with India's discomforts, eating spicy and sweet foods. Lee gives herself to the irresponsible Gopi in a bid to assimilate India and only ends up being disillusioned. Margaret falls a victim to India's deathly disease—jaundice. The Europeans find physical dangers like pollution, unhygienic conditions, dirty streets, heat and dust all round and these seem to bear down on him.

The "Westernized" Indians are equally removed from the real India. They live their opulent lives, intermix with the westerners but are naive about the real India. They introduce a kind of pseudo-culture in their homes by having lavish food and music no one listens to, donning clothes to the point of being overdressed, adopting nicknames, aware mostly of being like the westerners themselves. Despite tall talk by this class, typified by the lady politician, no real effort is made to improve and preserve the true values of India. The middle classes, like Gopi, lack the confidence to do anything. They are merely concerned with entering the right circles that will ensure an easy life in the quickest way possible. They are sensitive about their shortcomings and conceal them in temper-tantrums.

These complexities of Indian life are what Jhabvala has herself listed in her essay "Myself in India." Her last novel on India *Heat and Dust* further expands on her exposition of how India works on European nerves. In the parallel stories of Olivia and the English narrator the dilemmas of the West towards the East seem to emphasize what has always been and what will ever be. India is treated with the same suspicion, as being a den of thieves, unscrupulous people, by the Saunders's in Olivia's story and the English neighbour that this young English girl meets on arrival in India. India's dirt, food and water are all to be treated with care. Olivia at first shuts out the "heat and dust" in her tastefully done up bungalow. But soon she finds the isolation stultifying and ventures into that heat and dust of India which bogs her down to her doom. She hopes to absorb this India that is a mystery and is led into the exotic, rich but sinful world of the Nawab who involves her in a liaison that spells her unhappiness. The English narrator also leaves the safety of the mission and goes into the heart of India living in a room above the bazaar in the home of an ordinary Indian clerk, Inder Lal. She adopts the Indian way of life, living on vegetables and curd bought in the bazaar. She lives unencumbered by furniture in the Indian way, to the disappointment of her landlord who believes that English are synonymous with power and authority and should be seated on chairs. This English girl finds the Indian way of living disorderly. In the joint family she learns that the mother-in-law enjoys an enviable position for it is only as mother that a woman in India gets her due place. Inder Lal confesses that he cannot speak as freely with his wife who had been chosen for him for her fair complexion and appropriate family background.

But the narrator is also drawn into a sexual union with Inder Lal and is pregnant like Olivia. While Olivia has her child aborted, this girl in a different era is bold enough to have her child. But both cases indicate that to the Indian male the English girl is one of easy morals and they have proved themselves to have been so.

India is hot, dirty, overcrowded and diseased to all Europeans. The apathetic attitude of Indians to all life is beyond the understanding of the western mind. Their lack of aestheticism is horrifying and contrary to the Indian principles of cleanliness that the western mind finds baffling. The English narrator finds what had once been Olivia's elegant bungalow stuffed with furniture, the walls stained with betel juice and nothing of the garden left.

The young westerners who come in search of peace enthusiastically surrender to everything Indian but before long fall victim to India's diseases—dysentery and jaundice—grow weak and derelict and reach a stage when they find everything comes full circle and the west finds the east beyond its reach.

As elsewhere in her work, Indians are portrayed in their garish tastes for dress. The Rawul adds majesty to his position by dressing in princely garments, with plume, crest, *et al.* The Rani too is in flowing silks, chiefly to beguile the Americans with pomposity and exotica. Lindsay, the mother of Michael and Harriet, is "fascinated by the Rani—by her wonderful Paris clothes and Oriental jewellery." Although she and her children own property like "Propinquity" and much more, their lifestyle by contrast is frugal.

IV

Even while Kamala Markandaya and Ruth Prawer Jhabvala poignantly reveal the tensions that underlie East-West relations, one can say that both have a tragic vision. The tugs and pulls of culture, disparities in social patterns, economic differences become the third dimension of their stories. Firstly, they further the construction of the plot in their stories. The protagonist often finds himself in an abyss confronted by these seeming invincibles. He must overcome these differences. The differences do not rear their heads all of a sudden but work in an undercurrent till the mesh weaves closely around the lives of the protagonists. Artistically they provide the *raison d' etre* for the hero to extricate himself from this situation. The ways of his extrication vary from novel to novel. In Markandaya often there is compromise, which perhaps is her own attitude to fears and doubts of an expatriate position, so that the whole is really cathartic. It is also a psychological effect that she affects. Compromise itself is an easy solution but her tragic vision of racial tensions elicits her concern about them. There is also a concern in her for the misery of the poverty-stricken masses in India which her expatriate status naturally enlarges. As both Markandaya and Jhabvala have purportedly written for western audiences, both develop social and cultural celebrations in India with over-enthusiasm and extravagance, making it a focus for irony and humour or a picture of gloom and constraint. Both the authors, by their special position of being in a country other than their own, have imbibed a ready and detailed knowledge of the culture and social values of each society. In Jhabvala the earlier novels are generally social comedies that do not allow the differences to escalate into a conflict. But the perspective of the later novels changes to the mood of her own exposition in her essay "Myself in India." Like herself her western protagonists assert themselves and return to their old ways. He may be said to override the compelling circumstances that are in this case Indian influences. A change to return to his old self means an abandoning of the effort to understand. The bridge is still to be made, so that the novels end at the same point as E.M. Forster's and cry out "Not Now."

It must be said to her credit that Jhabvala has explored the complexity and subtlety of Indian society, its labyrinth of the Hindu undivided family and the tensions that arise out of the old and the new, East and West in a sophisticated way. In the earlier novels she never favours the young rebels or the old conservatives completely. The young are confused, naive; the old are self-deceived and disillusioned. These novels may be said to fall into pure social comedies in which the plot is designed to ensure happy endings and the emotional temperature is kept deliberately low. But in the novels commencing with *Esmond in India* the conclusions are left in mid-air or on a note of interrogation with problems unsolved or perhaps insoluble. So that like Markandaya she seems troubled by the divisions in humanity. Their stories acquire a lasting value which flowers from their tragic vision. They seem committed to the belief that wrongs must be righted. Insofar as there is latent optimism, the solutions are possible.

NOTES

1. T.G. Percival Spear, *The Nabobs: A Study of the Social Life of the English in 18th Century India: 1932.*
2. Romila Thapar, *Ancient Indian Social History: Some Interpretations* (Delhi, 1978), p. 30.
3. Ruth Prawer Jhabvala, *How I Became a Holy Mother and Other Stories*, p. 11.
4. *The Illustrated Weekly*, 15 June, 1979; Book Review by Nissim Ezekiel.
5. Ruth Prawer Jhabvala, *How I Became a Holy Mother*, p. 9.
6. *Ibid.*, p. 13.
7. *Ibid.*, p. 9
8. *Ibid.*, pp. 12-13.

The Language Tussle

The Indian writer in English performs the impossible task of communicating Indian modes of feeling and expression in a language, as Raja Rao puts it, "that is not one's own."[1] As a language, English was first introduced into India by a resolution of the Governor-General in Council Lord William Bentinck on March 7, 1835 "for the promotion of European literature and science among the natives of India."[2] It may have been designed to turn Indian taste and opinion in morals and intellect to an English one but the proliferation of English education in India made English the living speech of the Indian intelligentsia. English today is no longer a foreign language defined as being "not one's own though one may have a good knowledge of it . . . used for absorbing the culture of another nation" and used as "an alternative way of expressing the culture of one's own."[3] English has acquired the status of the second language, "one's own though not one's first in order of importance nor usually the first to be learnt."[4]

Creative writing in English began with the exposure of educated Indians to English culture and art forms. Borrowing the form of the novel from English literature Bankim Chandra Chatterjee wrote in 1864 his first novel in English, *Rajmohun's Wife*. He reverted however to writing regional-language fiction till at the turn of the century, Indians made the supreme "personal sacrifice," in the words of Babu Sambhunath Mukherjee, to write in English without which "no impression could be made in the camp of our British rulers."[5] That sacrifice has now reaped reward when many novels are being written in English, reaching a far wider audience amongst all the English-speaking peoples of the world. The point in question is whether these writers of Indian fiction in English have been successful in the projection of its Indian quality. In the words of the noted Hindi writer Sachchidananda Vatsyayana, "what is unique in our experience . . . can find expression only in an Indian language."[6]

The Indian writer in English has what B. Rajan calls his "mixed allegiances" and "the mixed sensibility." Primarily his facility with the English language enables him to write in English. At the same time his grasp over the vernacular makes it imperative to wrestle with and tame the English language, refashion it, indeed almost invent a language to capture Indian tonal rhythms. His own sensibility is really impure, being neither wholly one nor the other but a product of the two cultures to which he is naturally exposed. It makes him cosmopolitan but also rootless. He also holds a slightly detached view of his own society having "experienced the oriental's adjustment to a western society and readjustment again to the oriental."[7] This achievement he must express and only the west can understand and appreciate it. So he uses a language the west can understand. But this language is abstracted from the context of the living Indian culture. Even though the writer himself is fluent in English and has a mixed sensibility, most often he is writing about people "who do not normally speak or think in English."[8] Creativity will depend on rendering convincingly the idioms and nuances, the idiosyncracies of regional or linguistic speech, habits, to provide consistency between speech and character for maintaining that illusion of reality. The writer in English must mould the English language. Some English writers of fiction also faced dialectical problems which they solved by language arrangement. In his historical romances, Sir Walter Scott made his characters speak a neutral kind of English, neither medieval nor nineteenth-century speech. Thackeray solved it by his exquisite imitation of eighteenth-century speech and tone in *Henry Esmond.* Dickens sometimes used spelling devices to render the speech of his Cockney characters and Mark Twain introduced colloquial Americanisms in *Huckleberry Finn.* Early British writers on India, convinced that Indians could never really master English or English sensibility, imbued the dialogues of their Indian characters with malapropisms, mixed metaphors, twisted idioms, absence of articles and question patterns at the level of syntax. They believed that blood and race instincts showed themselves in speech. Indians writing of Indians in English are not concerned with making such implicit assumptions regarding social characteristics. Nor are they concerned with exploiting the English language as a dialect for producing a comic effect. English is the language in which they have chosen to reflect with utmost fidelity their whole range of sympathies and affections for things Indian as well as foreign. The Indian writer in English endeavours to bring upon his work a certain Indianness in the sum-total of description, narration, reflection, modes of thinking, ways of observation and other instinctive responses of people whose awareness has been conditioned by a language other than English. It is in this context that David McCutchion feels that English as a medium may work as "a barrier against real insight into the Indian mind and circumstances."[9]

Indian writers in English no doubt face obvious limitations when using English to write Indian fiction. There is a confused and restricted range of "registers" that they must confine themselves to, and which necessarily attribute to a lack in originality of style. Ruth Prawer Jhabvala, though not Indian but writing only of Indians except for her last novel, *In Search of Love and Beauty*,[10] has listed these obvious difficulties inherent in Indian fiction in English. In her short personal essay, "Moonlight Jasmine and Rickets" she states that "when one writes about India . . . and in English (as I do) inevitably one writes not for India but for western readers. Problems of communication present themselves, how to translate the idiom of one language into another, how to present a scene to an audience unfamiliar with its most obvious ingredients."[11]

Yet it is not an "act of self violation,"[12] as V.S. Naipaul suggests, because Indian writers in English have successfully proved that "English is flexible enough to accommodate any experience."[13] R.K. Narayan has proved that without experimenting with the English language, and only by its skilful use, he can delineate people whose responses and actions have no relation to this language or its habitual speakers. Raja Rao, like the Nigerian writer Chinua Achebe, has proved the compatibility of English with the spirit of the native language. By introducing subtle tonal values and syntactical devices of Sanskrit and Kannada into English, making literal translations of Kannada idioms, phrases, turns of speech, oaths and imprecations, he provides the rhythm and feel of rustic Kannada speech. Mulk Raj Anand makes abundant use of literal translation from Punjabi or Urdu in the dialogues of his characters. Khushwant Singh too recaptures faithfully the gestures, attitudes and the lingo of Punjab villagers. Bhabani Bhattacharya began with linguistic innovations and experimental coining of words, but failed in the attempt only because such words had no basis in either English or Bengali. He soon forsook the device, to write more successfully simple correct English in the manner of Narayan but continued handling curses as ineffectively and ludicrously as Mulk Raj Anand.

The language of Indian fiction in English operates, one may say, at two levels. First, there is the language of the non-English speaking Indians. This language must be assumed to have been translated directly from the vernacular into English. It may consist of translated words, images and phrases, occasional transliteration and sometimes syntactical differences to emphasize tonal rhythm. The other level is the spoken English of the English-speaking Indian, reported directly. This language is often governed by a limited "register," that situational segment of the English language governed by the range of vocabulary and syntax particular to the occasion or to the person who speaks or is spoken to. Each such "register" denotes effectively the quality of speech or the speaker. Linguistic innovations occur in such "registers" because it is the natural result of language interaction developed, as Nirad C. Chaudhari explains, out of "the linguistic basis of modern Indian culture."[14] Contact with English wrought changes in the regional language, making it "a combination of English, a denatured written vernacular and a mixed colloquial language."[15] The syncretistic quality of English in turn also made it vulnerable to regional language influences of tone, rhythm and vocabulary. The hybridization of English was reflected in collocations and compounding of words of the first and second languages. Syntactical differences marked this "register" as the rules of grammar of one language overlapped the other. The English of such speakers is therefore full of distortions and queerness; its "half-English, half-Indian" character may be funny but as Kamala Das says, "it is honest. It is as human as I am human, don't you see?"[16] Thomas Pyles has also asserted that this kind of Indian-English is "as legitimately English as that form of the language which happens to be spoken in the mother country."[17]

Over and beyond these two levels is the author's own mastery over the language, one of varied "registers." These then are the general patterns of English as they occur in Indian fiction. We shall now attempt a study of these general trends in the novels of Kamala Markandaya and Ruth Prawer Jhabvala to assess whether they have successfully met the challenges of language and theme.

II

Kamala Markandaya is an expatriate writer, living in London. Born and educated in India her personality has developed within the Indian cultural ethos. Markandaya at the same time has an enviable mastery over English. What is being sought to be examined is whether she meets the constraints of language while defining the varied characters in her various Indian novels and the Indian atmosphere.

While handling dialogue the author must be aware of the level of the speaker. In Indian novels in English, one level may be of those without any knowledge of English whose dialogue is assumed to be a constant translation from the vernacular. This is the level about which Mulk Raj Anand confesses that he translates "the dialogue in my novels from my mother tongue."[18] The other is that level of speaker who does speak English, may be in an adept way or may be of a kind that is strongly influenced by the vernacular whose idioms he borrows and translates, whose syntax he imposes on the new language and whose words he uses freely for want of an apt equivalent, in transliterations and collocations. There is a third level that is over and beyond these two levels—the language of the writer as narrator.

In her very first novel, *Nectar in a Sieve*, Markandaya has made her heroine Rukmani give us a first-person account of the tribulations she has borne like a Hindu Job. Rukmani had been taught by her father "to read and write." (11) Married to the tenant farmer Nathan at the age of twelve, it is only in the early stages of her first pregnancy that "With the leisure I now had, I took up writing again." (11) Rukmani must have had a rudimentary education in the vernacular so that her narrative must be assumed to be a translation of the original. To suit the limits of the character's credibility, Markandaya has effectively contrived at short, simple sentences, even though they be flawlessly intact in syntax. There are a few literal translations as when her new friend Kali is chided by the others for letting out Nathan's secrets. She should have "her mouth stitched," (6) they say. When Rukmani kept worrying about a male child, she was "putting lines" (18) in her face. Like most women novelists, Markandaya generally makes lesser literal translations. The translations that do occur are of those Indian delicacies that would have been more effective in transliteration. Dubious descriptions such as "wheat cakes fried in butter," "rice-cakes," "crisp golden pancakes" or even "bread and pancakes" are both inadequate and ineffective. There are transliterations in the book that are taken care of in the glossary provided at the beginning of the novel. Attia Hosain and Zeenuth Futehally also supplied a glossary of kinship and other Indian terms considered unfamiliar to the reader in their books *Sunlight on a Broken Column* and *Zohra* respectively. Markandaya goes a step further to explain some other terms in the body of the narrative. She shares this with Santha Rama Rau in *Remember the House*. We have Rukmani inform the reader that little Ira called Nathan "Apa" which means father. (15) Later when Ira is married and is seen coming home with her husband, Rukmani quickly traces "a colam, a pattern in white rice flour" (49) to welcome them. "Deepavali, the festival of lights is a festival mainly for the children but of course everyone who can takes part. I twisted cotton into wicks, soaked them in oil and placed them in mud saucers ready to be lit at night." (54)

Rukmani's language however is not always sustained in its simplicity. Despite the rambling manner in which she elaborates on transliterations or the slow manner in which she tells her tale and evokes pathos, Rukmani is never as realistic as Raja Rao's illiterate grandmother Achakka in *Kanthapura* whose expressions are not always literal translations from the Kannada language but are masterful uses of everyday images and thoughts common to most of Indian villages. Achakka refers to her neighbours by special characteristics that define them, such as their house descriptions or their places of occupation.

Rukmani, when she loses a young son, expresses the numb shock most poignantly in a simple lamenting and an incomprehensibility at death in one so young: "He was not very strong they told me. They merely laid hands on him and he fell. As if I did not know how thin and brittle he had grown? But why should others lay hands on him? They told me, but I could not remember. They repeated themselves again and again, but I kept forgetting?" (89) But at the death of Old Granny, Rukmani's philosophy on death raises doubts. Her bleak history is incapable of expressing such subtle wisdom. Discrepancies in language quality, therefore, do not make Rukmani as credible as Achakka. Even Rukmani's collocations are compounded in a way that has long passed into English such as "nose-screw," "water-buffalo," "dung-cake" and "bullock-cart." Except for "rice-water" we do not find in Kamala Markandaya any of Raja Rao's ingenuity.

In her second novel *Some Inner Fury*, Markandaya is on surer ground. Though this is also a first-person account, the heroine, like Markandaya herself, is well-born and well-educated, in love with an Englishman and thoroughly conversant with the English language. With considerable ease, therefore, Markandaya captures the pretentious English of Indian social climbers in pre-Independent India. She has no need to tailor language to a specific use and Markandaya's "uniform case of public-school English"[19] is quite in order. Transliterations are few and unlike the first book there is no glossary appendixed but Indian terminology is explained in the narrative, as when Mirabai's brother Kitsamy ties the necklace "thali" around his wife's neck that "would make her his wife." Kanya Kumari is elaborately defined as being the same as Cape Comorin. "Pappadams" are not given an inadequate description but there is a marked innovation in Indo-English collocation in descriptions such as Kit having the "England-returned stamp" as his "senior-uncle" thinks. Mirabai can quite convincingly say that Kit had returned "fresh from an English spring" (32) but "had wilted with the heat." She discovers "a colony of young green snakes" in the river to which they drive with Richard for a swim. If Mira speaks a convincing language, her mother speaks an English which is not always right at the level of syntax. When asking her son Kit about the choice of a bride, she makes that common Indian mistake of converting an assertive into an interrogative: "The girl pleases you?—you think your mother has chosen well?" (56) Only the old relative Dodamma's declaration that servants can "eat you out of house and home" (62) is out of key with her personality.

In her third novel *A Silence of Desire*, the omniscient narrator gives a third-person account of the fissures that develop in the smooth relationship of Sarojini and her husband Dandekar. Dialogue in this book is far-ranging from the chief characters through Dandekar's colleagues to the little servant-girl. Dandekar being a petty government official should have a limited "register," a restrained expression. His conversations with his colleagues are direct and simple. A senior colleague Ghosh has a more varied "register" and can forcefully denounce the Swamy in a tone of authority. Dandekar's dialogues with his colleagues may be taken as original. Sarojini's and Dandekar's dialogues with each other can be of either level because they speak a convincing tone and idiom. Indian idioms like "this or that place" occur quite naturally in Sarojini's speech. There are collocations like "temple-sari" and Sarojini has a treasured photograph in her trunk that held her "two special-occasion saris." Dandekar must content himself with "lime-rice" when his wife is away from home. These expressions only add to the argument that Sarojini and Dandekar may be said to belong to either level of speakers. Where Markandaya fails in the dialogue in this novel is in the speech of the servant-girl. A servant in India never talks to an Indian master in English. Her speech must be treated then as translation. If so, it is an ineffectual treatment. "Mistress gone out. Mistress not say . . . telling me look after Chandru baba and gone up. . . . Chandru baba giving trouble sir, calling his mother, crying in lie down" (9) indicates a kind of butler-English which cannot be said to be in consonance with her character or situation. Missing infinitives and articles or using the present continuous are features of this brand of English. Later when Dandekar is down with shingles she cries: "Oh sir, your face. It's come up red like pomegranate seed like the pox it is, sir," (176) is another example that neither leaves her here nor there.

Sarojini's language has collocations and a few transliterations which are in the manner of the earlier novels well-handled in the narrative and their meaning made explicit. "To you the *tulasi* is a plant that grows in earth like the rest," (87) she tells Dandekar who does not pray to it but believes "it was a symbol of God." (5)

Markandaya is most successful in handling dialogue in her fourth novel *Possession*. In the first-person narration, an Indian author Anasuya tells us the story of Valmiki's life from the time she meets him in a South Indian village till his growth as a renowned artist in London and even America under the patronage of Caroline. Anasuya, like Mirabai of *Some Inner Fury*, is like Markandaya herself. The author can therefore write the dialogues in her smooth easy English way so far as Anasuya's narrative is in question. But it is in Valmiki that she really meets her challenge and quite successfully.

At the beginning of the story Valmiki has no knowledge of English so that Anasuya translates all his Tamil communications with her. He may be placed at the lowest level of what B.B. Kachru refers to as "a cline of bilingualism." Valmiki progresses step by step along this imagined scale, running from absolute monolingualism at one end, through varying degrees of bilingualism to absolute ambilingualism at the other end. In the beginning, Valmiki speaks to Anasuya in Tamil. Learns to say "no" in English. Two years later in London when Anasuya meets him he speaks a kind of

"Butler-English," only a slightly improved variety. "I see her. Not blind. You well? Make safe trip to London?" (50) he asks Anasuya. At this stage he has not yet learnt to use the auxiliaries properly. Anasuya comments: "He speaks in English, a curious laconic English with an accent hovering between Tamil and Arabic—all the tortured s's, the 'p' sounds for 'f' of the first, the rolling r's of the second and little of the fluency I had somehow expected . . . his English had come in scraps from India, England, his travels, and I could not help surmising from the cook houseboy on the ground floor." (50) Valmiki at this stage still translates directly from his first language—Tamil. To Caroline who asks him if the Swamy meant a great deal to him he says:

> "Yes. He was like father and mother and friend. Always good. Always help."
> "Help? In what way?"
> "Many ways."
> "Buying you things? In that way?"
> "That way also." He frowned struggling to be fair to her and at the same time to him.
> "But he not rich like you, not buy much. Few things, few times." (52-53)

In structure Valmiki's English is strongly marked by the features of Tamil. At this stage, it hovers between substandard English and Tamil, being structurally deviant. Statements are turned into questions: "Then you not know from letter?" (51-52) There is a total absence of auxiliaries and determiners: "He say good, I feel good. He say work for god, I work for god. He say you paint well, I paint well." (52-53) His vocabulary too is extremely limited. He demands to know the meaning of "crevice." He cannot read and even though Tamil may have been easier, he sticks to talking in English. When Anasuya returns to London once again Valmiki is speaking a fairly good English. He is able to rebuff Anasuya's comments that his costume is outlandish with: "My dear, you know and I know. But how many of the people here can tell sheep from goat?" (108) After a slight peregrination into beastly art Valmiki turns once more to spirituality. He now talks philosophically with Anasuya. By the time the final break with Caroline comes he has graduated along the cline of bilingualism from absolute monolingualism to practically the ambilingual point, reflecting the normal progress that an Indian makes in order to gain competence. Valmiki's language rings with the same credibility as Mrs. Peabody's English. This English housekeeper who meets Anasuya at Lady Caroline's house after a long time greets her with: "But seeing you there like, it fair gave me a start." (78) Even the Italian landlady's remarks at Annabel's going away: "There is of her nothing left" said Emilia practically. "The window is open—pouf, she is gone. You throw away the old cage, you get for yourself another bird, soon everything is fine. Yes." (203) Markandaya is therefore very successful in this novel adopting the tonal rhythm, vocabulary and expressions of the English language spoken differently by speakers of English from different parts of the world.

So far as Indian speech characteristics go, apart from Valmiki, she has captured well the limited "register" of the English-educated Indians like the village school-master. Interpreting for Valmiki in the village, he informs Caroline: "Madam, he is thinking: where I am to get dye-stuffs for picture?" and also that "he says his wish to paint all the people in one face." (47) Valmiki resorts to translating from the Tamil expressions that formed a part of his life in the village. It had been a hard one for him and all he was served was "one hand of rice and water." (59)

Transliterations follow the pattern of the older books. Wherever they occur they are followed by explanations that form part of the narrative. The small child in the village that pointed the way to Caroline and Anasuya "cupped his hand for baksheesh." (21) Caroline who lingered on in the village had to be provided with four "ravikais" to supplement a change of blouses. The boy Valmiki could not leave his home to travel with Caroline during "raukalam," the dark period during which it is inauspicious to undertake anything of note. (29) Valmiki was directed by the Swamy to go to the "ashram" that "would shelter him as it would shelter anyone who needed it, and its religious foundation would ensure his safe-keeping." (35) The "Swamy" has been described as a true Indian ascetic unlike a Christian parish priest or a missionary or a revivalist not concerned with keeping tabs on a human being to plot his spiritual progress. His whole aim is to achieve detachment from the world. In the face of these transliterations, Markandaya's habit of calling Indian delicacies by inapt English equivalents like "a platter of crepes as big as dinner plates and as fine as the finest lace" (167) seems unwarranted and unnecessary.

In *A Handful of Rice* the vagaband hero Ravi, like Rukmani in *Nectar in a Sieve,* has a bit of learning: "He could read, he could write—not only the vernacular but English." (27) Unlike Rukmani, it is not Ravi who tells us his story but the omniscient narrator. Markandaya is therefore not shackled to the constraints of language in the same way as in *Nectar in a Sieve*. But in the dialogues of Ravi and the others, Markandaya is treading dangerous ground. Ravi's dialogues with his wife Nalini, his friend Damodar, and his other relatives may be taken as translations. But some of his thoughts that have been translated by the narrator have over-reached the limitations of a street urchin's thoughts. They are too English in content such as Ravi's "if all you had was one rupee between you and kingdom come." (9) The sophistication of the idiom cannot make it applicable to a boy of Ravi's standing. The author seems trapped between the needs of language and character. At another time Ravi deplored the attitude of the haves towards the have-nots thinking that "the big memsahibs down to the would-be memsahibs, petty little squirts like this one (Jayamma) who was a petty tailor's wife: all of them, who called themselves respectable and bamboozled you into falling down in worship." (19) There are occasions that redeem such writing. For example, when Ravi complains to his young wife Nalini that the scantily-clad English memsahibs tantalized him but, he says, "they look at me as if I were made of wood." (155)

For the first time the transliterations are not accompanied with explanations: Indian terminology like "Chatram," "chapli," "masala dosai," "idlies," "pattani," "banchots" and authenticity like the "police-thana" and the "water-buffaloes."

The Coffer Dams is also a third-person narration. Markandaya has been provided ample scope to write her brand of English in the dialogues of the English experts and Indian technologists who are the main characters in this novel. The English characters pose no problem at all and it is the dialogues of the Indian characters that needs to be examined. There is Gopal Rao who has some knowledge of English but allows the principles of his own vernacular to influence this English. He may be placed on the second level in the scale of bilingualism. The determiners are missing in his English as can be seen when he says: "Aid to underdeveloped countries is not a free gift, there are strings attached to it, for instance all our equipment here, we have to buy from Britain with our loan." (66) Gopal Rao reminds one of Nikhil in Anita Desai's *Voices in the City*. Gopal Rao misses the object of his verb when he says to the same English technologists ringed around him, "Not only we, you also have taken from others. Like Elgin marbles . . . or Koh-i-noor which is biggest diamond in the crown of your queen—which you took from us and never paid for it." (66) This aspect of English grammar is the hardest for foreigners to master. Gopal Rao omits articles, uses "also" instead of "too" besides repeating the noun phrase after a relative clause, all common errors that Indians on this scale of bilingualism chiefly make. Krishnan the engineer in *The Coffer Dams* is like Raghavan the young I.A.S. officer in Anita Desai's *Voices in the City*. He comes more or less to being at the central point on this scale because of his competence in the use of one or more "registers" in English. Krishnan has a good mastery of the official "register." His range however is extremely limited, often causing him to err when dealing with more sophisticated speakers of English.

At the lowest point of this cline is Das the butler who may be compared to Valmiki in his early years in *Possession*. His kind of English has no tense modification or the normal structure of English. The "ing" forms are used as finite verbs; negatives are formed without the auxiliary "do." His conversation with his English master may be taken as an example:

"Where's Memsahib"
"Memsahib telling gone, jungle, sahib"
"Already?"
"Yes sir, gone early," said Das, "for trapping birds."
"Birds? Are you sure?"
"Yes sir master. Gone with jungly mens." (80)

Das has picked up his English in bits and pieces from his English masters and mistresses during the pre-independence days. His English is therefore credible. Like him is Jackson's boy who shouts out, "Coming saar" when called for. A little higher on the scale is the Indian official minion who surveys the angry Rawlings to answer for the loss of equipment with: "My dear sir, ten thousand tons of equipment are passing through our hands each day. From Rome, Cairo, Moscow." (74-75) He has only his official "register" like Shanmugan who believes: "We shall keep face also, phase one of our project being completed on time, the country will sing our praises. Is this not good for all of us." (152)

There is only one transliteration "Molaga, thanni sahib, the pepper water master" which in the pattern of the earlier novels is neatly explained in narrative. *The Coffer Dams* is, as Uma Parameswaran states, "a turning point in her literary career and has deeper implications in the context of expatriation."[20]

In *The Nowhere Man,* Srinivas and his wife Vasantha have been expatriates in London for a long time. Their language is far removed from the Indian language context so that the problems of East and West cannot occur. Nevertheless Markandaya's own expatriation has afforded her the chance to come to grips with the problem confronting expatriates and she has solved the problem of being away from Indian idioms to the betterment of her art. In Laxman telling his father: "You are a dark horse" or "Now where did you meet her eh? Come on now, tell all," (181) we have the new generation Indian far removed from his heritage talking another language. Srinivas remembered that he had never spoken to his father in this way.

In a later novel *Two Virgins*, the tone and idiom in the language of Saroja is inconsistent with her sensibility. The full purport of Markandaya's expatriate dilemmas can be clearly understood in the abundance of anglicized idioms. Amma for instance, chiding Appa for blaming the English in India for all the present ills, says he is "riding a hobby horse." Saroja, through whose consciousness we make the observations, thinks that people "traipse up North" to the Ganges. Saroja is not exposed to this degree of English vocabulary. Nor can she think that Lalitha is her "trumpcard." Amma even utters words like "codswallop" and "basilisk." Lalitha's disappearance is referred to as having "catapulted herself out of the orbit of the community." Chingleput the "good sweetmeat and pastry cook" is little Saroja's confidante. These little discrepancies mar the effect of the language of this book. Amma's dialogues are otherwise simple statements that maintain the tonal rhythm of the vernacular from which it may be deemed translated. But there is a dearth of Indian imagery and Appa's "sufficient unto the day" sounds inappropriate in the setting of their village life. Transliterations of words now readily familiar with the English go without further elaboration like "nimbupani," "chup," "jaldi." But the more uncommon South Indian words are followed by explanations in the pattern of the earlier novels. Lalitha is called "mundi, obstinate." Aunt Alamelu makes "ginger kayasam, a concoction of crushed ginger root and sugar and spice infused in boiling water." Saroja wears a "davani" which went on top of her blouse and was dropped over her breasts in "gathers and folds."

In *The Golden Honeycomb*, Markandaya is fairly safe in her handling of dialogue. This saga of a princely family assumes that the speakers are ambilingual or at least on way to becoming so. Bawajiraj II has had an English education from English tutors. His consort Mohini's and his mother the Dowager's dialogues may be translations but their language lacks the flavour of local idioms the nuances of the regional language in rhythm and tone. If their language is inconsistent in character that of Janaki, the gardener's daughter, is even more out of keeping with her standing in life.

The dialogues echo Indianisms only in the transliterations. It is only the first and the last novels of Markandaya that carry a glossary or footnotes of such Indian words. What is not explained in the footnotes is explained, as always in her novels, in the fabric of the narrative. When Bawajiraj I dies, his widow Manjula strips herself of all her jewellery except the "thali" explained as "the necklace with which she has been wedded." (27) Before Bawajiraj I was appointed ruler of Devapur, the British had selected a stooge who was unfortunately a "bania . . . a merchant of the Vaisya caste." (5) The "punkah-wallah . . . was supposed to keep the infernal air circulating (those ridiculous petticoats strung from the ceiling)" while "the sloth in a turban pulled the ropes that swished them around." (202) Rabi explains that "a goonda . . . is no worse than a looter." (289) Rabi the illegitimate son of Bawajiraj II can inherit only his mother's jewels that "descend in the female line" as "striddhana" till the Viceroy can approve of his total inheritance. The other transliterations are taken care of in the footnotes. But Lady Copeland's telling Janaki to stop crying in Hindustani, "Chup raho? Jao jaldi jao" (183) perhaps redeems the language shortcomings in the dialogue in this book only because it strikes the notes of realism. So does the Ayah's "Sophie missie, missing Sahib" or "No you worry yourself memsahib. Outdoors girl doing bad things." (183)

The festival of Holi is described at length by Rabi in the course of conversation: "A very jolly festival. . . . Though its religious too. . . . A little worship and a lot of hurling things about . . . water mostly . . . coloured water and various powders . . . and flowers and rice, all sorts of missiles. They pelt you like demons. . . . Everyone's equal on that day . . . and it is absolutely forbidden to take umbrage." (459)

The other point of examination is to see whether the language meets the requirements of theme in Markandaya. The language is of the West and the theme of the East. If the English language must undergo some change from its conventional use to suit Indian speech, it must also be suitably amended to meet the ends of theme. This can be done only if idioms and imagery are adopted to the Indian theme and context. Environmental descriptions and moods and purposes can also be defined through language devices. It requires a certain amount of creativity in the writer to explore the latent possibilities in language that can take it beyond its limited passive use. By doing so, creative writers can liberate themselves from fettered expression of selecting metaphors that are far-ranging. Aristotle's statement that "the greatest thing by far is to have a command of metaphor. This alone cannot be imparted to another: it is the mark of genius,"[21] is carried through in Markandaya's "search for perfection of expression in alliance with a significant theme."[22]

In her first novel *Nectar in a Sieve,* Markandaya uses the imagery and metaphor picked from Rukmani's peasant environs and experience. Nathan before his marriage is "as brittle as a bamboo before it bursts into flames." (6) When the peace of the village is disturbed by the clamour and din of the tannery, she wishes it away like a bad dream, thinking of a peaceful life beyond. But Nathan knows that there can be no return and advises her to "bend like the grass that you do not break." (28) They soon find themselves deprived of the land on which they worked and in anguish Rukmani's mind "turned this way and that like a paper kite, dipping to every current of air, unsure of its meaning." (134) Finally they leave their homes to "wander like jackals" in the city where they are robbed of their meagre belongings and Rukmani promises to be more wary. Nathan's "After the horse has bolted?" (149) intrudes in an otherwise well-adopted language; it is too anglicized for an Indian setting.

Spiritualized by her suffering, Rukmani acquires a biblical quality. Fate bludgeons her, not her mistakes. Like Job she has entrusted herself to God's care and speaks on occasion a language reminiscent of him in its repetitions and archaisms. She watched in consternation as the paddy "grew and grew" and the flood waters "rose and rose." enlarging and emphasizing her experiences. She introduced Kenny to Nathan in third-person deferential because it was through his medical treatment that God worked, she feels, when she has a son. But now, "Four more sons I borne in as many years" she confesses so that Dr. Kenny cheers Nathan with "You have begotten five healthy sons." (37) When one of these sons joins the strike for better wages "to eat our fill and to marry and for the sons we shall beget," (64) it is beyond Rukmani's meek submissive nature. Rukmani speaks in slow, measured tones that suggest her quiet resignation.

David Lodge says that "repetition is the first step towards offering an account of the way language works in . . . novels."[23] In this novel the constant repetition of negative forms in "There was no money left. . . . Nothing left to sell. Nothing to be had from my efforts . . . nothing left to sell," (79) or Nathan dying near the gutter where "Nobody gave anything, nobody had anything to give" (185) provides the leitmotif to the overwhelming despair in the peasant who must "work without hope," collecting nectar in a sieve.

But there is a poetic mastery in the language of this novel. When Rukmani is forced to use wet wood for fuel during the deluge, she hears the fire burn "hissing at the water in the wood." Similarly walking the rain-drenched city roads Rukmani felt the "liquid mud come squelching up between my toes as I walked." Both impressions are tactile and onomatopoeic.

In *Some Inner Fury*, the narrator is an educated sophisticated girl, like the author herself. Mira's secure background provides the first metaphors with a tranquil feeling. There is no inconsistency in the poetry of the language that Mira uses to describe the river and "the silver river sand sloped in ripples and waves as the cool weather water had left it" (37) in the days of her blossoming romance with the Englishman Richard. But that love is doomed and it is portended in the "Darkness" that came "striding over the seas towards us." Mira's country dominated by Richard's is brewing rebellion exploited in expressions of claustrophobia. Kit has loved an English girl but submits to marrying Premala, the Indian girl of his mother's choice, locking "the coffers of his thought" and standing "vigilant before them." (57) Mira's love for Richard cannot attain its logical end either: "the oppression was building up once more, the air was heavy and still, it was like trying to breathe under a blanket." (269) There is hostility all around on the fateful night of the Government House party so that "the darkness closed over you like water . . . darkness closed round like a wall." (228) The "life blood of love" was sucked by the vampire of their "unadmitted truth; that no relationship could exist in such animosities."

Markandaya moulds language appropriately to harmonize the concept and execution of her idea. When Kit and Mira rush to the school to search for Premala, they find the school on flames over which the sound of rain is heard in the repeated sibilant "S": "There was a slight sound from the darkness, swapping wind and rain and the hissing flames." (241) Premala is found dead and in the ensuing melee Kit too is killed. His death brings the years "like ashes in my mouth," confesses Mira. Earlier when Richard tells Mira he has to go away, she feels: "The happiness of a moment before seemed a mockery. Capped and belled it jeered at me," evoking the image of the jester whose business it is to mock and jeer.

The prose is clear and seemingly artless in *A Silence of Desire* but the vocabulary is chosen with the care of a craftsman. Although metaphor is not as wide in its range as in the previous novels, there are some streaks of suitable imagery. Sarojini's cousin Rajam "was a sunny disposition tiring only those who liked a little shade with their sun." (14) The ill Dandekar, confused by the turns in his life, looks at "the stupidity of the flies that fell like sluggish suicides into the lazy open jaws of the golden geckos on the ceiling." (185) Dandekar's thoughts go round "like a squirrel in a cage." He wonders why he has to suffer and is compared to a "dangling blind."

Silence is signified in the calm, placidity and efficiency of Sarojini who "did most things placidly . . . from this calm proceeded the routine and the regularity that met the neat and orderly needs of his nature." (7) Without her there is all noise; the children squabble, Dandekar must raise his voice; there is fretful whining, nerves are frayed. Dandekar seems to live surrounded by noise in the office and at home. With the increase of noise around him he withdraws into a shell of silence: "some kind of capsule seemed to have formed about him through which the world had come filtered and faint." (109).

The Swamy has his own silences communicating through thought rather than words.

Sarojini's religiosity comes through in the mention of the "tulasi" she worshipped and the "gods and goddesses singly and in groups" which Dandekar liked but could not describe in detail. The discovery of the Swamy's photograph had disturbed him emotionally and showed the cracks in the foundations of his life. Strongly rooted in the firm foundation of his marriage he searches for those roots like the banian tree roots "hung from spreading branches striving to touch the soil, to earth themselves and begin new life" (220) after Sarojini's operation.

In *Possession*, the theme of East-West tension is kept constantly before our eyes. There is an apt repetition of the word "possess" and the verbs used to express his desire to hold, keep, exploit, claim, crave, dominate, mould and caress. The metaphors have little to identify them as being particular to the Indian scene. A writer culls images from personal experience. Markandaya does not live in India permanently and this shows in the lack of an instinctive derivation of metaphor. There is instead a wordiness that obscures significance. The tenor is not clear and the medium becomes turgid as over-emphasis of theme robs the narrative of subtlety.

In *A Handful of Rice*, the sentences are short and crisp but the metaphors are sparse. This story of the basic facts of earning a living requires the solid precision of language to project such an experience. Nouns and verbs build up the mundane structure of everyday life and the comic as well as tragic moments of life are realistically described. The "pattani" seller trying to balance his tray, the sensation of being poised perilously in an inclined rickshaw-seat, Ravi's efforts to gain some privacy on the terrace of an overcrowded slum-house, the common tap, are brought out in the choice of language.

The theme is conveyed through the repetition of keywords and imagery. That keyword is "rice," symbolic in Nalini's winnowing the rice mixed with chaff and stones. Ravi is concerned with keeping his children chubby and the store-room filled with rice. Apu discusses the price of rice with Ravi's father. Finally the frenzied mob loots the granary "driven by the same fear, screaming and fighting in the contaminating rice-frenzy." Other images are symbolic of restriction and restraint. Memories of bad harvests are like the "slimy tentacles reaching out to clutch at him." (205) In Ravi's city home "silence dragged on like barbed wire stretching between them." Economic disparity is emphasized in the alliteration: "The sensuous sumptuous, unthinking display of wealth for the unthinking wealthy." (237)

According to Mark Schorer, metaphors sometimes strain towards symbolism and thus form the basis of structure in a novel.[24] In this novel such an image is "the jungle" which in its symbolic role "expresses in a memorable form one of the main themes of a literary work."[25] Ravi compares the city to the jungle where "its darkness, its lawlessness where a man's strength and courage alone gave him mastery . . . live by jungle law, and then see who survived." (33) To unemployed graduates "the city was a jungle. . . . A man-made jungle—full of snares and traps." (209) In the context of the jungle theme, the novel has animal imagery. Damodar prowls the city by the night. Ravi carries tailored clothes to various houses like a human donkey. It is the derogatory nature of this animal terminology that stresses the overall pessimism implied in the symbol of the jungle.

Markandaya's poetry is discernible in expressions like "hate guttered away like a cheap candle," or in those "tight wound coils of feeling," "the fretfulness of existence" or even in Nalini's' "black hair had inky blue lights" in it.

The purpose of metaphor is to see the basic issue with greater clarity inspired by mental pictures that are analogous to the idea in mind. In *The Coffer Dams* there are several vivid metaphors that are indicative of the strained relationship between the English and the Indian engineers. Metaphor and simile help to delineate character. Clinton is religiously attached to his work so that his "plans sang a psalm in his mind." Bashim loves to operate the crane so "contentment sat like a pearl in the centre of his forehead." Krishnan's strong will is emphasized in plaiting his fingers "like over lapped wattle, which does not give or break." Mackendrick tries to keep good relationship between Indians and whites but comes in "lowing defeat like an empty trawl." Racial prejudice occasions metaphors like obstacles. Clinton and Helen have little in common, "as if they were walking on different levels, he on the flyover, she on the underpass." Millie tells Helen that to get on in the East, "stiff little fences erected by silly old women afraid of the rape of their minds" were essential. This flare of metaphors indicates her quivering sensitivity to feeling, the range of Markandaya's experience and the vividness of her imagination.

Markandaya uses relative clauses in this novel as independent sentences presumably to create the necessary tension "by imparting a certain continuity and a feeling of breathlessness as a result of the speeding up of the narrative"[26] as K.C. Nambiar suggests. Clauses such as "which slid stealthily along the wall to the switch and snapped on the light as she came in" (143) or "who understood motion, national force, but was unable to pass on his understanding" are really stylistic devices of the Tamil literary tradition. Indian languages repeat the verb phrases in confirmatory and echo statements. The use of reduplication of relative clauses as independent sentences and transitive verbs without violation of "the finer rules of English idiom and grammar," according to F.W. Bateson."[27]

But the language in this novel also echoes poetry . Drums are heard "in the troughs of the tossing forest," the throbbing is like "an echo in the air." Henderson "became aware of something in the air and groped for it, clumsily like a drunken man after a nimblefly, for this was not his forte, and at length touched a tenuous wing."

In *The Nowhere Man*, the description is of thought rather than action and an inclination for verbiage diminishes the dramatic effect. Many of the metaphors in this novel spring from anguish over racial tension and the terrible lack of tolerance it implies. "Imagery is a powerful weapon in the stylistic arsenal that she commands to project the theme," (192) suggests Margaret Joseph. Colonialism and racialism, under the thin black skin of Abdul Zanzibari is "jampacked" with "memories of flags that had followed the spice trade." Srinivas remembers "the poor man's rattling bones" and links it to the fat profits that accrued to the West. He represents the coloureds "whose running sores and ulcerated interior time could not heal" after repression by the English overlords. Markandaya's poetic mastery over the language comes through "in the very teeth of Quit and Vamoose notices, among the ice floes, he saw the colours of humanity, pity and concern in the greens and blues and hazels and grays of island eyes for this stalking stranger that alternating between hunch back and straight spine was himself." (181)

David Lodge says that style "is the very medium in which the subject is turned into art."[28] In *Two Virgins*, this style is one of conversational reportage that fails to project vividly what has been felt and therefore shows little evidence of art. The language is simple but the simplicity betrays superficiality. The animal world provides a frequent vehicle for images that are little more than surface comparisons. But occasional images such as the wind that made the sugarcanes clash "with a sound like the rattling of sabres in a cinema saga" are the little "joyful secrets."

Images of richness and splendour are repeated in *The Golden Honeycomb* in the word "gold," "golden," "amber." Such language denotes wealth and luxury in all its forms. More than half of *The Golden Honeycomb* is written in the present tense, thereby conveying some of the freshness and immediacy of actual contemporary experience. Once the episode with the mill-hand Jaya is over, the narrative switches to the past tense. Historical accounts are craftily worded to convey a devastating irony. Style changes according to the point of view and is moulded to the character's thoughts to portray varied temperament. Thus Bawajiraj, Rabi or the Dewan become more real in the manner in which they think rather than the manner in which they speak.

Kamala Markandaya has an instinct for effective use of language. Torn apart as she is between the country of her birth and that of her adoption, there is an ambivalence in her that becomes her stylistic experiments.

III

Ruth Prawer Jhabvala, European by birth, English by upbringing and education and Indian only by marriage, has the required objectivity to look around her and observe detachedly the Indian people, the Indian atmosphere, the Indian sensitivity. Unfortunately her purview is a limited one because she writes of people whose language and sensibility have been modified to a small extent by English influences. It gives her an advantage nevertheless because she writes in English of those who speak English or have a hybridized sensibility. She can perhaps understand this small section and therefore has been quite successful in the aspect of realism that marks her fiction. The narration is chiefly in the third person, *Heat and Dust* being a parallel narration in the first- and third-persons and *A New Dominion* being constructed on epistolary and alternating first- and third-person accounts. While the narrator employs a single "register" in omniscience, dialogue is also presented dramatically in which two or more "registers" seem to be operative. These varied "registers" project the peculiarities of characters and situation highlighting thereby the comic tone. As Meena Belliappa observes, "her dialogues catch the vernacular flavour to some extent and reproduce its idiosyncrasies of speech through the peculiar nuances of Indian English and more often through a literal translation of the vernacularisms."[29]

Jhabvala, having centred her stories on this English-speaking section of Indian society, has taken care to place them on their different levels of the assumed "cline of bilingualism." An Indian in her stories speaks an English that is influenced greatly by vernacularisms in vocabulary, syntax, tone and rhythm. He translates idioms from the vernacular literally and makes curious collocations. Some of her characters are those who do not speak English and whose dialogues may be deemed wholly translated. There is a third level of speaker; one who has a technical knowledge of English and applies it rigidly to the spoken tongue. Their language sounds pompous and ridiculous in the informality of the setting. A closer study of her novels will elucidate this.

In her first novel *To Whom She Will,* Radha is the widow of the England-educated barrister-turned-freedom-fighter Nirad Chakravorty. Her father is an anglophile barrister and her daughter Amrita a convent-school and elitist-college product. Radha's social background suggests her familiarity with the English language but it is just a social pretension. She often makes use of literal translations of idioms to press her point. Duly disturbed by Amrita's reluctance to obey her on issues she is heard telling her sister Tara, wife of the rich Vazir Dayal: "Am I to sit at home and eat my-two-three chapaties alone and talk to myself like an old woman?" (34) She confesses, "The girl is eating my life up. Why must I be so punished?" Amrita's marriage is very much on her mind but "such a beautiful fair girl like my Amrita, I would not let her go to just anybody." (127) So she urges Amrita that "to go to Lady Ram Prashad you will please wear the green one of chiffon which I bought for you." Radha's dialogues suggest that they are directly translated by herself from the vernacular into English. This distorted syntax is a common feature in such speakers of English. When Amrita's hairstyle does not meet her approval she reverts to translating an Indian idiom: "A hundred times, I have told you, why do you not change your hair style." There is no interrogation in the sense, only in the style. She urges Amrita to accompany her to Lady Ram Prashad because "Lady Ram Prashad said specially, please bring your Amrita, I have not seen her for a long time." (24) Direct speech is mixed up with the indirect. Radha's mission in life is to find a husband for Amrita who must be "well-educated, of course, England-returned I would like, and he must have a good position, an I.C.S. or a gazetted officer." The collocation "England-returned" is typically Indian in origin. Radha's speech besides is one in which articles are inadvertently dropped. When her lodger Krishna Sen Gupta calls to the servant for a cup of tea she informs him that "he has gone to bazar." The Indian tone is well-reflected in Radha when she persuades Krishna to postpone his trip to his parents in Calcutta: "Tomorrow you can go if you wish, what am I saying, today even: with my own hands I will pack for you your two or three miserable little pieces of shirt." (189) It is further stressed in the syntax and rhythm of her anxious concern for Krishna Sen Gupta when he has yet to write her a letter of safe arrival. "But this Krishna Sen Gupta now—would you think it is the behaviour of a gentleman, England-returned not to write to those who are anxious even, 'I have arrived safely,' on a post card?" (264) The relative clause is framed wrongly, as is the whole structure of the sentence.

But it is not Radha alone who errs with the language. Even her convent-educated daughter resorts to the mistakes of translating directly from the vernacular. She asks her mother: "Why can you never understood one no, Mamma?" (99) Hari Sahni, with whom Amrita fancies herself in love, comes from a refugee family settled in Delhi. His mother does not appear to be English-speaking so that her dialogue is rendered in translation, syntactically correct but adopted in tone and rhythm. Her request for "one glass water" or her blessing to Amrita, "May she wash the faces of a hundred sons" (172) are cases in point. Hari lacks Amrita's background and education. He falters with the object of his verbs as when he asks her if she would like to see the new film: "You want Amrita?" In this case the form of the interrogative is also not right. His Amrita is "the nightingale of my heart, the stars of my eyes, the juice of my liver." (145) His excuse for not keeping an appointment with Amrita's father was: "My sister was not very well in her health last night. I had to fetch the Doctor, that is the reason why I did not come." (139) It is the "register" he is familiar with in his working life and which he feels compelled to use as the best in a social commitment. Even the highly sophisticated Lady Ram Prashad makes syntactical errors. "But unfortunately some ladies are coming to my house, just now they are coming." (160) Sarla too defaults in the use of possessive pronouns when she says "Husband has gone away."

The converting of a statement into an interrogation with only an inflection of tone is quite common. Radha asks Tarla: "Your headache is better?" in a manner that commands, not merely demands to know. When Amrita leaves her grandfather's house before lunch her servants query: "you are not staying to eat in our house."

Transliterations are few and typical food items are inadequately explained in English. But on occasions she resorts to transliterating in an ironical manner as when Hari punctuates a serious discussion of his love-affair and marriage with taking a "laddoo" and eating it. But Hari sits down to eat his dinner of "gram and vegetables and curds out of little brass bowls on a tray." Such garbled versions mar the effects of transliteration which can sometimes enhance the effectiveness of style. For instance, Radha is tired of her sister Tarla's "committee-shommittee."

In her second novel, *The Nature of Passion*, the *dramatis personae* of the story is listed at the beginning, in which "Phuphiji" is described as Lalaji's sister, Lalaji's daughter Nimmi compares with Amrita of the earlier novel and speaks Amrita's kind of language. Unlike Amrita's family background Nimmi's is an up and coming family in which the westernism has just begun to be aped. Lalaji's language is crude just as his officer son's language is refined. Transliterations like "pan," "kurta-pyjama" and collocations like "foreign-returned," "gazetted-officer" provide Indianisms.

Shakuntala in *Esmond in India* is like Amrita of the first novel and Nimmi of the second. Like them, she has an affluent background modified by a college education that gives her a certain amount of westernism. Her language too has been affected by the interaction of the vernacular as that of her genteel mother Madhuri and Cambridge-educated brother Amrit's wife, Indira. Syntactical influences of the first language, hybrid collocations and occasional translations and transliterations form her language and that of the others.

The commonest form that the syntactical difference takes is changing assertives and negatives into questions by mere inflection of tone. These are tonal rhythms reminiscent of the first language. When asked for a suggestion on a wedding gift for a friend of India,

Shakuntala asks: "She plays tennis? She swims? She laughs a lot and smokes cigarettes?" (12) To her father she says: "Someone is coming to see you?" (14) Surprised that her father Har Dayal's real mentor in fashion and fun at Cambridge had been the freedom fighter Ram Nath she asks: "He wore English clothes?" and wonders about his sister "Uma auntie? She is also very different now?" (31)

Indira's language is similar. Unsure if Shakuntala will really accompany her on the shopping spree she asks: "You will be ready by eleven? You are coming?" Neither is the genteel chocolate-drinking Madhuri different. About the present, she asks her daughter-in-law: "How much do you think to spend?" which hints at a direct translation of the vernacular. To her daughter Shakuntala she says: "At least you can give them to press?" using "press" instead of "iron" and in a form that can only suggest its being a noun. Annoyed with Shakuntala's persistent playing of the gramophone she complains: "for one hour now she has been playing" cliding the object of that verb. To Ram Nath's wife she boasts that Shakuntala has "begun social life" and gone out with English ladies to Agra. "Later perhaps we will send her to finishing school in Switzerland together with the daughter of Sir Homy and Lady Fonwala—you must be knowing?" omitting necessary articles and ending a statement converting it to a query. Lakshmi too is a victim to these errors. On her visit to Madhuri when told that she has a headache, she at once solicits: "It is aching? I will tell you excellent remedy—please only put your feet into cold water," ignoring articles, making a mess of the question form as in a later "Your sons are also well-settled?"

Transliterations and collocations are a natural phenomenon in language interaction. It is quite common for instance to hear children call their parents's friends "Uncleji" and "Auntieji" in which the Indian deferential suffix "ji" is added to make the parental address less informal. Shakuntala, a product of this hybrid culture, therefore uses such terms of address. It is also a common practice in Indian English to follow the vernacular pattern of addressing uncles and aunties first by their name then by the term of address as Shakuntala says, "Uma auntie." In the case of transliteration Jhabvala adopts Markandaya's technique of providing explanations in the narrative. When Bachani, Uma's old maid, reports to Gulab her daughter that the mother has gone to her brother, Gulab provides the Indian term "mamu" for the maternal uncle. Or when Lakshmi bemoans her "Pitaji," her husband Ram Nath is irritated by this sudden mention of her father. When Gulab's little boy Ravi draws his "Nani's house," his father Esmond tells him that "after you've drawn your granny's house, will you draw your own house too?" The Englishman Esmond's language is flawless by comparison. The Swamy's *Padmasana* pose in Yoga is explained as "his legs tucked under him, his feet on his thighs, his hand palms upwards on his knees, his eyes wide open and unblinking, stared straight through her." The *Sirasana* is similarly explained as a great Yogic exercise in which the spirit mingles with the Infinite. Other words like "kurta-pyjama," "dhoti," "atta," "dal," "ghee" are simply transliterated but Jhabvala, like Markandaya again, refrains from calling Indian food by its rightful name so that we find inappropriate equivalents like "horserandish pancake." But there are other expressions like "Har-Dayal, Par-Dayal" that make up for these deficiencies.

In *The Householder*, speech-patterns follow the trends of the earlier novels. Statements are converted to questions like Indu asking Prem, "We are going?" or Prem asking the bridegroom, "I think you don't feel so well?" Often direct translations occur as when Prem asks a student, "where are you looking?" The pretentious Mrs. Khanna, the Principal's wife, deplores the speed at which the fan is being turned and says "Its on very fast." There is the usual dropping of articles as when she says: "People with cold should be careful to cover their mouths" and like when a lady guest requested to sing says: "I have cold today." The article does not feature in vernacular and therefore it is found to be a common lapse in Indian English. The same kind of lapse is noticeable in the sentence-structure when Prem tells his friend Sohanlal, "Now a days I cannot afford so much to go to the Cinema, or in Indu telling her landlady Mrs. Seigal, "Here I have done no knitting wool is so costly to buy." There is the usual cliding of the object in Indu's "He gives, but what does he understand of what things cost." She makes the same mistake at the Principal's house when refusing the *laddoos* with "I don't want." Translations of entire phrases are made as when Mrs. Seigal tells Indu, "when a girl is married she thinks and thinks of her father's house" or when "everything goes round and round" in the pregnant Indu. Mrs. Seigal gets her son out of the way when exchanging Indu's confidences with "you're my good son."

Wrong usage of "also" and "too" and the jumbled order of words form the pattern of the Principal Mr. Khanna's speech: "I too am interested in these questions." For the first time Indian food gets its rightful name in this novel when Prem's mother asks the servant if he knew how to make "muli-ki-roti" and Indu craves for "samusas" from the bazaar.

So far, the women in the stories had one kind of "register" that was linked to their role as housewife or social creature. The male characters too had their own "register" of a man-about town, an idealist or connected to his role of a bread-winner. In Mr. Chaddha's talk at the Principal's tea-party we can note his pompous use of language: "A sense of comradeship . . . that will survive and triumph over any buffets of fortune that it might be our fate to encounter." (102) It smacks of Victorian propriety and its ponderous moral tone. It differs significantly from the other social "registers" as also from the narrator's "register".

In *Get Ready for Battle*, Vishnu, Mala and Kusum speak in the same style as the characters in the previous novels, in which articles are dropped, infinitives are made short of and statements are converted to questions. Kusum's "Does anyone give him massage?" or Vishnu's not wanting to go to Bombay "Because I don't want" and Mala's "Thank you such clever women it is nice to read about in the newspapers" are cases in point. Jhabvala has made the significant addition of a new rhythm of speech and its tonal quality in the dialogue of the Anglo-Indian woman come to buy furniture from Som Nath: "You give us for twenty-two rupees and we'll take." (101) The socialite Mrs. Bhatnagar, like Lady Ram Prashad of the first novel, is also prone to syntactical influences of the vernacular. "We have come here on important business and there is still left much to discuss." Vishnu's mother Sarla Devi speaks in a similar fashion asking Gulzarilal her husband, "You have bought the land next to Bundi Busti?"

In *A Backward Place,* there are more European characters so that Jhabvala's own English may be freely used. The handling of dialogue in the context of the East and the West is therefore considerably minimized. But we find the pompous "register" of Mr. Chaddha echoed in the revolutionary Jaykar whose paper *Second Thoughts* reflects the same verbosity and moral tones. If we compare this "register" with that of Mr. Gupta, we can hear him say "All are waiting for me in the office" and the Indian girl in his suite "came to remind me for Sunday. Sunday there is a family function." The preposition is not used. Even Bal who has an English wife trips up with "Do you think my brother would ever allow," omitting the object.

The inclusion of English characters in more numbers continues in *A New Dominion.* But there are enough Indian characters to provide a challenge to the writer in English. The bearer warns Raymond that the voice "is not speaking nice language." The Indian student Gopi tells Raymond that "whatever I want, she (Asha) buys for me." The Indian lady-minister in a bid to couch any obscenity says: "women who are carrying." Raymond's servant Shyam brings his "cousin-brother" for a certificate because "Only they want like that. For nothing. Just you name, Sahib." Transliterations follow the pattern of the earlier books of being expanded in explanations.

In *Heat and Dust* the technique of the parallel story offers a first-person narrative and a third-person narrative. In Olivia's story the Nawab of Khatm tells Olivia: "I will sent for it immediately" referring to a piano-tuner. Despite his close associations with the English he makes mistakes in his tenses, changes sentences into questions as when he says to Olivia: "If I have them (the pianos) repaired and brought upstairs you will come and play for me Olivia?" (92)

In the young narrator's story Dr. Gopal the Medical Superintendent at the hospital asks her "which country you are from?" (115) And in continuation "you saw the type of patients we have and then also we make mistakes on our side, how is it to be avoided. I would like to have more staff. I make applications in triplicate." (116) Transliterations like "hijra" are explained like the other transliterations of the earlier novels.

Three Continents uses only a sprinkling of Indianisms. These are chiefly by way of nomenclature, "Bari Rani" and "Babaji," terms explained in subsequent phrases. The volunteers are *Bhais* and the yogic term "neti" is adopted by the twins to substitute "phoney."

Ruth Prawer Jhabvala's handling of dialogue of her Indian characters tends no doubt to get monotonous because they follow the same trends. It is inevitable because it stems from the same social setting, at least in the earlier novels. Because of its setting such dialogue adds realism. But if Jhabvala had merely done this she would have been accused of mocking the Indians amongst whom she lives. She had enhanced the Indian quality of her novels by her art of invoking environment to delineate character, crisis or conflict in human relationships. Let us now consider how she handles atmosphere and theme.

Her first novels are social comedies in which the ironies exist in the given situation. Her first novel *To Whom She Will* takes its theme from the *Panchatantra* that advocates marrying a girl in tender age or she gives herself "to whom she will." Amrita the girl in question is the daughter of the late freedom fighter Nirad Chakravorty and Radha the oldest daughter of Pandit Ram Bahadur Saxena who was a well-bred anglophile. His "voice was precise, the accent pure English" and he had many English friends. His drawing room is "shut in by pieces of heavy English furniture and a clutter of tastelessly chosen objects d'art" which were all brought back by him from his trips aboard. The family eats at "a broad heavy dining table . . . spread with a gleaming white cloth and laid with initialled cutlery." But they ate "curried vegetables with cutlets and curds and chapatis followed by a mountain of very white rice and chicken curry." Juxtaposed is the refugee family of Hari

Sahni, Amrita's colleague at All India Radio and the man she fancies herself in love with. He lives in a cramped tenement in which the noises of the street, the radio and the running water from the tap pervade. Hari Sahni ate his dinner "on a charpoy" out of a brass tray and bowls. While he longs to acquire Amrita's westernisms and is apologetic about his lifestyle, Amrita is eternally grateful to him for forgiving her those westernisms which she tries to shed and begins eating with her fingers. Radha who had at one time forsaken all her riches to fight for freedom is well-poised to conquer the bastion of Hari Sahni and therefore "dressed in her most expensive sari, a metallic blue Mysore silk, with an elaborate border and wore almost all her jewels." The description is vivid, detailed so that her overdress is "very splendid if a trifle barbaric." But Hari's family decide to marry him to Sushila Anand who is more like them. Hari is elated about his impending marriage though at the same time he is making elopement plans with Amrita. In this and subsequent novels Jhabvala exploits the ironies of Indian ways and delineates their characters because most of her earlier novels are all social comedies where Indians try hard at being a little English and can come only a little way. Her next novel *The Nature of Passion* takes its theme from the *Bhagwad Gita* in which "*Rajasa* is to be of the nature of passion giving rise to thirst (for pleasure) and attachment. It binds the embodied by attachment."[30] The atmosphere of wealth and a passion for it is built up in the character of Lalaji and Dev Raj. The ironies lie in the character of Kanta the daughter-in-law of Lalaji who wants none of his crudeness but lot of his money to help her keep her children in boarding school and provide her an annual holiday, or in the painter, dramatist and journalist who attach themselves to Viddi for his money.

It is with her third book *Esmond in India* that the first traces of boredom in the Indian landscape come through. There were so many things in India that Esmond found difficult to endure any longer. As an Englishman he loved aesthetic living and kept a smart "little dining table in his smart little dining corner." But his Indian wife Gulab prefers to sit and eat on the floor, rich, spicy Indian food brought to her by her mother or the maid, which she eats with her fingers till she has licked her fingers clean. She never accompanied Esmond to his parties where "It gave him the opportunity implying that real Indian ladies from the best old Indian families still stayed secluded at home." Though his foreign friends are thrilled at the thought "of veiled women sitting together in marbled courtyards where fountains perhaps splashed and sprightly maid-servants engaged them in bantcring conversation in between singing love lyrics to the lute," (42-43) India was really dull; nothing but the road running through the dry, barren and anonymous landscape. When they came to a village it was always the same village, as dry and dusty as the surrounding landscape. Sometimes they ran the gauntlet of a row of village-shops in which there was nothing to buy except the things the poor sell to the poor, wilting vegetables, lentils, soiled sweetmeat, weak tea in brass tumblers. Imperceptibly, dust unto dust, village and shops faded again into desert landscapc and sometimes there was a ruined mosque among the withered shrubs and stumps of trees. The sun became hotter, hotter every minute, making of sky and earth one vast white bowl of dust." (144) The pervading smell of spices and strong perfume seemed everywnere "filled with dust and germs and too much sweetness, in the faint but penetrating smell of over-ripe fruit." Esmond's English sensibilities could not accustom itself to these strong smells, and the heat and dust or the "Indian sky an unchanging unending expanse of white blue glare, the epitomes of meaningless monotony which dwarfed all human life into insignificance." (252)

This was the real mystique of India that Jhabvala continues to project through subsequent novels. In *The Householder*, the ironies inherent in the role of a middle class householder in India are highlighted in language that suggests the impossibilities of living to this ideal. In *Get Ready for Battle*, the characters of Gulzarilal and his wife Sarla Devi are juxtaposed in language that suggests humour and irony. Gulzarilal with his newly-acquired wealth has "largely adopted a western manner of life; but when he was alone, he still liked to sit on the floor and eat his food from little bowls with his fingers. And he still adhered to the breakfast of his youth, to lentils and fried puris and hot pickles in little dishes." (26)

A Backward Place carries forth in similar images of beggars and dust and crowds the ironies that exist in India. Outside Etta's flat beyond the cottages were the homes of India's poor: "No sound came from it, no smell except of dry dust. The sky seemed equally endless and desolate." (119) In the new housing colony for government servants Jaykar's son lived in a flat that was like the others "new, identical, their yellow plaster was peeling off, their ledges were sagging and there were cracks in the cement work." There was no adequate provision for electricity and water. The buses were crowded; every time a bus came, they surged forward and the stronger got on and the weaker were left behind. But Judy the English wife of Bal liked being here: "It was busy and crowded and at the same time peaceful. This was a paradox. . . . One left the house and everywhere it was full of people, so much going on; little shops in which women bargained, men played cards on a bed pulled out into the street, students studied under a lamp-post, holy men cried Ram Ram tapping with a long staff and rattling a tin, and film songs came out of a radio: yet always, above everything, the sky was large and beautiful, and one had only to look up and it was peaceful." (222)

In *A New Dominion* the impressionistic images of over-crowding in buses and the heat-smells and discomfort become more pronounced. Raymond's description of the scene from his room-window is thus: "In the courtyard next to that another woman fights with her servant who doesn't fight back. He is an undernourished boy who looks eight but is probably twelve. . . . Every one here eats excessively . . . those that do eat." (3) A recurrent image that is oft-repeated in Jhabvala's stories is that of the Indian practice of sitting crosslegged on the floor instead of on chairs and the general dismissal of furniture. Her Indian characters are constantly rolling out mats to sleep on the floor. Another image that constantly recurs is that of the dead body being carried for cremation. In this book there is one very vivid description: "Women screaming inside . . . a crowd gathered outside. Men arguing and giving each other contrary instructions . . . several bent down to heave something up and place it on the shoulders of several others. The women redoubled their cries. Lee saw . . . they were carrying . . . a body on a plank. It was wound in a red cloth and secured to the plank with ropes; the face was uncovered. All the men fell behind the pall-bearers. . . . They walked . . . chanting as they went. In between chanting, they carried on fairly normal conversation with each other. . . . They got to the river and there the body was placed on the pyre and a priest said prayers and the fire was lit and the body began to burn." (11) The smells of India are conveyed in the smell of the poor who do wash but "don't have the opportunity to wash well, or change their clothes very often." Raymond notices that Indians do not have an aesthetic sense and finds the crockery chipped, cracks with dirt ingrained in them and a sofa with worn-out springs. Everywhere the landscape seems flat, bleak and dusty where trees planted would take a long time to grow. Flies and mosquitoes everywhere. An Indian is either under-dressed or over-dressed. The Minister wore a thick cotton saree and had fat bulging arms while Pam had earrings, bracelets, anklets, toe-rings and little bells inserted in her hair.

Ruth Jhabvala's impressions of India seem to linger on in the *Heat and Dust*, her last novel on India. The young narrator finds that the street at night has "each stall and barrow . . . lit up with a flare of naptha." There are crowds of people; some are sleeping—it's so warm that all they have to do is stretch out, no bedding is necessary. There are a number of crippled children, one boy propelling himself on his legless rump. People are buying from the hawkers and stand there eating while others are looking in the gutters to find what has been thrown away. She finds the same untidiness in Indian living as Raymond of the earlier novel observed. When the narrator visits her landlord Inder Lal's family downstairs, she saw it "was certainly very untidy. . . . Ritu swiftly cleared some clothes and toys off a bench." The bus she travels on is old and rickety, packed with people to bursting point and with luggage on top. The Indian countryside is once again flat land, broiling sky, distances and dust. Especially dust. The gardens of the old English bungalows are no "patches of open ground where the clerks congregate in the shade of whatever trees have been left." Olivia in her time had also observed these vast distances, the vast sky, "the dust and sun and occasional broken fort or mosque or cluster of tombs. It was so different from what one knew that it was like being not in a different part of this world but in another world altogether, in another reality." (89)

IV

V.Y. Kantak, quoting Remy de Gourmont, writes: "The art of writing is nothing more or less than the art of feeling, the art of seeing, the art of hearing, the art of using all the senses, whether directly or through the imagination."[31] Indian fiction writers face a special challenge while doing so. Markandaya and Jhabvala, the two authors under study, have dealt with Indians who either never speak English or do so only under special circumstances and pressures. There is also the proficient speaker of English in Markandaya's work and only minor roles of this category in Jhabvala. In the case of the two earlier kinds of Indians, the authors must use the devices of the English language to retain the integrity of their characters. Markandaya, we have seen, has been only partially successful in doing so. She has submitted to the needs of the language at the cost of expression. She makes scant use of translating Indian idioms into English but does not hesitate to intrude with hackneyed cliches and English idioms in the dialogues of her characters. There is therefore a confrontation of the language of the west with an Indian expression. Yet she retains some of the Indianness by infusing transliterations appended by explanatory phrases as a device in the dialogues of Indians with English listeners or as part of garrulity in a long-winded narration. But there are times when she avoids the transliterations substituting it only with an inadequate English equivalent. This reduces the effect considerably but is suitably made up in collocations English and hybrid. Compounding words is a vernacular device to take the place of a qualifying phrase and effects immediacy and realism.

Jhabvala by contrast has been more successful in meeting the language needs of her Indian characters. This has been possible because she has confined herself to writing about Indians who speak a certain variety of English in a given situation. It will be appropriate to mention here that Jhabvala, despite her western background, has mastered this "foreign" language of the country she writes about to be able to translate idioms from that language into their English speech. It gives her art the necessary element of realism when she engages in idioms such as "will steal the skill off," "dried up little thorn," "look like a sick cat" in *Esmond in India.* Her transliterations follow the device of being explained, as in Markandaya. The device forms part of her art when the explanations come from good bilingual speakers or at least knowledgeable ones. But she also shares Markandaya's flow of avoiding transliterations where they might have been more appropriate than the fuzzed English explanation.

Experiments with the syntax of the language also become necessary to introduce the tonal rhythm and typical responses and spirit of the speakers more adept in their mother-tongue. An attempt at changing the structure is more perceptible in Jhabvala than in Markandaya in whom we find its very limited use. By doing so Jhabvala has conveyed accurately the characteristic idioms of pride camouflaged as humility, of pomp covered up by surface-simplicity adding thereby to the extent of realism of her characters. She has confined herself to delineating Indians of a particular region only in and around Delhi so that there is no variation in the kinds of differences that occur in that syntax. It might have become monotonous because of sheer repetition but the "register" of the omniscient narrator breaks that monotony. Even so it does suffer from a little repetition. Markandaya gives no exact location to her novels nor do the syntactical differences she occasionally uses to mar her characters's speeches have any more distinguishing tonal rhythm to suggest any particular influence.

These devices are conscious efforts at turning language to an "Indian" use. There is another device that is a more spontaneous effort of the artist to record his responses to life through objects and events that are connected to experience. Art is a mode of expression as well as communication. Both Markandaya and Jhabvala have done well in evoking imagery that is Indian. Markandaya's metaphor stems from her pride in being an Indian and is often lush though highly readable. Her overriding concern is the subjugation of the East by the West and the East's near-rejection of the West's progressiveness. In novel after novel she negates this approach emphasizing that we are "made of the same clay." Imagery linked to the earth and words like clay, mud, brown are used repeatedly to become a leit motif. Difference of colour divides the human race and is the root-cause of this conflict.

In Jhabvala the inner tensions of being unable to merge with India in her lifetime is really because of the impact of the Indian summer day and heat. She confesses: "Only those who have lived through days of endless heat know their effect on one's behaviour." The appalling transformation in the characters, the crisis and conflict in their social patterns stem from this alienation from the environment. She stresses it in a recurring use of "yellow," "gold," "golden," "heat" and "dust," all symptomatic of India's stifling heat and oppression. With her western perspective, she views increasingly this growing alienation in her later novels. The ironies of India exist mostly on the economic disparities and a westerner is appalled generally by the poverty as it exists in India. She projects this in a style that H.M. Williams describes as "scaling down, toning down, subduing the Indian mess and violence and general complexity."[32] Jhabvala's descriptions of arid landscapes, crowded buses, the noises and smells of Indians are impressionistic. The two authors's styles are different, each having her own "manner of linguistic expression," but the characteristic style may be gleaned "in terms of diction or characteristic choice of words, sentence-structure and syntax; the density and types of figurative language; the pattern of its rhythm and of its component sounds and its rhetorical aims and devices."[33]

NOTES

1. Raja Rao, *Kanthapura* (Oxford, 1947), p. 9.
2. R.S. Singh, *Indian Novel in English* (New Delhi, 1977), p. 7.
3. Quoted by P.E. Dastur, *Sarojini Naidu* (Mysore, 1961), p. 50.
4. *Loc. cit.*
5. Quoted by N.C. Kelkar, "Letter to Meredith Townsend," *The Mahratta*, Poona, Feb. 1901.
6. *Udyog Mandala* (Kerala, Dec. 65), p. 4.
7. M.E. Derrett, *The Modern Indian Novel in English: A Comparative Approach* (Brussels, 1966), p. 152.
8. Meenakshi Mukherjee, *The Twice-Born Fiction* (New Delhi, 1974), p. 167.
9. Ramesh Mohan, ed., *Indian Writing in English* (Hyderabad, 1978), p. 42.
10. Ruth Prawer Jhabvala, *In Search of Love and Beauty* (London, 1983).
11. K.N. Sinha, ed., *Indian Writing in English* (New Delhi, 1979), p. 156.
12. V.S. Naipaul, *An Area of Darkness* (London, 1964), p. 215.
13. John Bess, *Commonwealth Literature* (Heinemann, 1965), p. 123.
14. Nirad C. Chaudhari, *The Autobiography of an Unknown Indian* (Macmillan, 1961), p. 486.
15. *Loc. cit.*
16. Kamala Das, *The Old Playhouse and Other Poems* (Orient Longman, 1973), p. 26.
17. Thomas Pyles, *The Origin and Development of the English Language* (New York, 1971), p. 238.
18. Mulk Raj Anand, *The Kind Emperor's English or The Role of the English Language in Free India* (Bombay, 1948), pp. 23-24.
19. Meenakshi Mukherjee, p. 170.
20. Uma Parameswaran, *A Study of Representative Indo-English Novelists* (New Delhi, 1976), p. 85.
21. Stephen Ullmann, *Language and Style* (Oxford, 1966), p. 201.
22. Margaret P. Joseph, p. 157.
23. David Lodge, *The Language of Fiction* (London, 1966), pp. 83-85.
24. Margaret P. Joseph, p. 183.
25. Mark Schorer, "Fiction and the Analogical Matrix," *Kenyon*

Review, Autumn 1949, XI, 4.

26. Ramesh Mohan, p. 170.
27. *Loc. cit.*
28. Margaret P. Joseph, p. 199.
29. Meena Belliappa, "A Study of Jhabvala's Fiction," *The Banasthali Patrika,* Jan. 1969, Year 4, No. 12, p. 80.
30. "Introduction," *The Nature of Passion.*
31. *Critical Essays on Indian Writing in English,* ed. M.K. Naik, *et al* (Macmillan, Madras, 1977), p. 224.
32. Haydn Moore Williams, *Studies in Modern Indian Fiction in English* (Calcutta, 1943), p. 147.
33. M.H. Abrams, *A Glossary of Literary Terms* (New York, 1971), p. 165.

Conclusion

The East-West encounter in its ramifications is the gist of Kamala Markandaya's and Ruth Prawar Jhabvala's writing. Living in the countries of their adoption but with their innate beliefs coursing through them, they realize the difficulties and impossibilities of a complete absorption. This neuroses takes the form of their art. The early Greeks had related genius to the spirit that haunts the artist until it is exorcised in the artefact. Giving body to those fears and doubts had a cathartic effect recognized by psychologists and subjective writers. It is only on the completion of such work that the author experiences a measure of freedom and relief. Markandaya and Jhabvala being of almost the same age, the former born in 1924 the latter in 1929, and being women have found enough in their experiences to keep the East and the West apart. But it is equally noticeable that underlying their observations is the optimism that an understanding can be reached. Each of these authors has stipulated her views on issues related to the East-West dichotomy. These views find expression in their novels.

To take Kamala Markandaya first. We find that in her paper "On Images," presented at a seminar on Socio-Literature held at the East-West Centre for Cultural Interchange in Honolulu, Hawai, in 1973, she discusses certain ideas that occur in her novels. She argues that human beings have certain preconceptions about people which find expression in certain images that influence behaviour with others. This attitude of an individual to another individual broadens into the attitude of a nation to another nation. In the days of the empire, Asians and Africans were spoken of in derogatory terms, springing from certain rigid ideas about them. This resulted in fixed images rising in the minds of others. The myth of the supposed low intellect of the African produced the counter-myth of the intellectual superiority of the whites. Moreover, the whiteman believed the myth that his race was the elect of God because the black man worshipped sticks and stones. This myth urged the white man to believe that he had a mission to fulfil, thereby justifying his exploitation of the country of his adoption. This assumed superiority produced a corresponding sense of inferiority in the natives. Colonialism led to a different scale of values for the whites and non-whites resulting in social injustice and the corrosion of spiritual values. Kamala Markandaya makes her novel the forum for her sensitive cries against suffering caused by such racial tension. Living in India through its struggle against imperial rule, Markandaya is still haunted by the memories of her colonial past. Living in a country that once dominated India and where racial tension is rearing its ugly head, Markandaya finds the problem of the ruler and the ruled ever-present before her eyes. In her novels, political confrontation of the East and the West is largely evident; the colonized harp on the exploitation they have been forced to endure and the colonisers on the amount of good they have done to the colony. In India, racial tension generated because of Britain's occupation of India or its enjoying the spoils is now nearly non-existent. The new and younger writers reflect the confidence and self-assurance of an independent country. But the simmering discontent at inequalities all round the globe, threatening disaster on a massive scale, fuels Markandaya's concern for universal equality. A new kind of thinking is necessary which will show people that there are factors common to both whites and non-whites. Horror, human intellect and philanthropy are found in all races. Other controversies are rooted in this basic premise of being unequal. By highlighting the tragedy caused by such inharmonious attitudes, Markandaya achieves, as perhaps she intended, a cathartic effect. Meenakshi Mukherjee considers Markandaya's talk of West and East with capital "W" and "E" as "dangerous abstractions" that are detrimental to "a particular and concrete realization of individual human experiences."[1] They may on the other hand be seen as T.S. Eliot's concept of "objective correlative" which because of its tragedy induces a negation and encourages the ideals and needs of a fruitful relationship. Turning to Jhabvala, her essay "Myself in India" is a revelation of her own inability to "merge" with India. Being a European and writing primarily for Europeans, her novels reflect the Europeans's predicament in India. The environmental hostility that the European is up against in India's tropical heat endangers his cool and quiet temperament hitherto nurtured in cool climates. The Indian sun makes him irritable.[3] Her own tensions and irritability get transposed to her European characters: "They yell at servants. . . . 'My God,' they ask, 'what's happening to me?' My Western characters who of course include myself have reason to be appalled at the transformation—their most cherished principles and feelings seem to be changing."

The other glaring anamoly that the European finds in India is its appalling poverty juxtaposed besides its wealth. Accustomed to the affluence of the West, Jhabvala and Markandaya are both acutely sensitive to India's grinding poverty. To the European Jhabvala what is particularly appalling is the apathetic attitude of wealthy Indians towards it. "Can one lose sight of that fact?" she queries. As a European it is not easy to accept the deplorable sights of the sick and the poor with equanimity or as sins of a past life. The belief of reincarnation cannot and does not come easily to a European. It can only be so if it is ingrained. In her opinion the only Europeans who can go through all this are doctors and social workers who by the very nature of their work will be less sensitive. Besides the heat and dust, poverty and sickness, it is the hypocrisy of the modern cultured westernized Indians that she finds disconcerting. Their "lively conversation" she feels is "not prompted by anything they really feel strongly about but by what they think they ought to feel strongly about." Their unconcern for a truly socialistic pattern of society in India is appalling to her. Unlike the Indian, the European cannot take refuge from these anamolies in religion and philosophy. Believing ardently in the virtues of conquering such deterrents in the way of a golden life, the passivity and stagnation that abounds in India in the name of religion and spirituality become a matter of grave concern to her. Her own expatriate dilemmas become the object of her comic vision and she comments ironically on what is and what should be. In her earlier books we saw her depict the scramble for acquiring riches, status and respectability by those forced to flee their possessions during the Partition. Social inequalities are seen resting on economic status, despite the ideals of equality generated by Gandhi's freedom struggle. In the earlier books there are no Westerners. It is the Indians themselves caught struggling with a western ethos and an Indian one. It is in the novels beginning with *Esmond in India* that the western characters appear and the author's dilemmas of expatriation find expression. The western characters are ranged against the hostile environmental background and they react strongly to it. There are some who attempt to adopt and absorb but reach a point when they feel they must close up. During their period of absorption they present a ridiculous figure. The Indian characters are always those who have assimilated a certain amount of Englishness and are of the kind that the author has seen at close quarters. She finds them only half-emancipated and makes them objects of her ironic study. It is not ridicule or condemnation of either side. But by highlighting the incongruities and hypocrisies in each. Jhabvala also aims at a catharsis.

The didacticism that both authors aim at takes the form of objective correlatives in the form of characters and situations. This gives their writing an artistic projection. Socio-literature tells what it is like to be there and feel it happening to you. The two authors have treated East-West personal and social relations with the same urgency that Forster attempted in *A Passage to India*. The impact of the West was felt in India in certain externals like sartorial habits but more intricately in certain attitudes to life and the world around. Markandaya explores the vital formative areas of individual consciousness that project the images of cultural change. She has an "uncanny gift of inhabiting the shifting landscapes of an outer reality with human beings whose sensibility becomes a sensitive measure of the inner reality as it responds to the stimulus of change."[3] Jhabvala's ironic vision sees in this change a defiance of old values, superficial and not of any seriousness or earnestness. In this context one aspect that draws attention is the projection of the Indian women by these two women novelists.

In Jhabvala, the Indian women are chiefly those who have undergone the impact of western culture. Through her own education she is made aware of her individuality. She has absorbed new ideas, tastes, and manners which she tries to bring into practice because she finds them attractive. But she is held back by the dictates of parents, brothers, friends or husband who maintain that she must keep up the Sita-Savitri image. She has been taught to seek fulfilment in her duty to her husband and to accept no man's love apart from her husband's. In case she cannot for some reasons abide by her commitment to her husband, she must seek fulfilment in spiritualizing or sublimating her feelings. The dual fidelity to her own wishes and that of her family results in a clash of cultures. The girls try to assert themselves but finally succumb to their elders. What they have experienced of the alien culture is superficial and lasts only till some crisis or experience in their lives jolts them back to the inherent culture with which they can identify easily and without much trouble. Jhabvala's heroines are all of the order. But some of Markandaya's heroines assert themselves in their new culture and do not succumb to their elders. Such girls like Mira, Premala and Sarojini only come to grief.

Another important aspect of woman that features in the authors is that of mother and mother-in-law. In Jhabvala's stories the Indian wife is a silent suffering woman and becomes a venerable figure only on becoming the mother of a son. As a mother-in-law she is never willing to allow the wife to gain a hold on the feelings of her son. The young bride who finds the adjustments difficult suffers her bitter and unhappy frustrations silently.

In Markandaya the mother image is glorified in the Indian tradition. A mother of sons becomes venerable and feels fulfilled while those with girls feel only a sense of loss. But with daughters the role of the mother is always a protective one. It is relevant to note here that the attitudes of the two authors may be seen in their own relations to India—one, a daughter of India and the other a daughter-in-law.

The artistic value of their writing is validated by their moral aim to right the wrongs. The solution lies not in total absorption but by overcoming strong prejudices out of a genuine love for each other as people. The integrity of both sides can be maintained so that the contact nourishes and does not overwhelm. The universality of the issue extends beyond the symbol of two disparate cultures, one pragmatic and rational, the other orthodox and traditional. Their coming together to modify each other is a lesson extended to all humanity. It is only with this spirit of give-and- take that any viable relationship can be established.

Thematically the novels have been validated but what adds to their literary worth is the use of language. Markandaya confesses that she polishes her sentences endlessly till perfection. One can attribute that exuberance in her language to her "Indianness"—a craving for colour, vitality and music. By its very quality it makes her readable to the point of enchantment. This is not to suggest that Jhabvala's language is any the less readable. It is of the restrained, tongue-in-cheek variety which evokes humour in a very subtle way which is indeed very English. What finer or more fitting way could there be to resolve the East-West encounter than providing in the style of the writing the unique qualities of harmony.

NOTES

1. Meenakshi Mukherjee, p. 83.
2. K.N. Sinha, p. 161.
3. A.V. Krishna Rao, *The Indo-Anglian Novel and the Changing Tradition* (Mysore, 1972), p. 67.

Bibliography

A. PRIMARY SOURCES

Anand, Mulk Raj. *Untouchable*. New Delhi, 1970. First publ. 1935.

———. *Coolie*. New Delhi, 1972. First publ. 1936.

———. *Seven Summers*. Orient, Delhi. First publ. 1968.

———. *Private Life of an Indian Prince*. Delhi, 1972. First publ. 1953.

———. *Two Leaves and a Bud*. Hind, Delhi. First Publ. 1937.

———. *Death of a Hero*. Orient, Delhi. First publ. 1963.

Bhattacharya, Bhabani. *A Goddess Named Gold*. Delhi, 1960.

———. *Music for Mohini*. Delhi. First publ. 1952.

———. *He Who Rides a Tiger*. Delhi, 1955. First publ. 1954.

———. *Shadow from Ladakh*. Delhi, 1966.

———. *Steel Hawk and Other Stories*. Delhi, 1968.

Brata, Sasthi. *My God Died Young*. Delhi, 1967.

———. *A Search for Home*. New Delhi, 1975.

Chaudhari, Nirad C. *To Live or Not to Live*. Delhi, 1970.

———. *The Autobiography of an Unknown Indian*. Macmillan, 1961.

Cowasjee, Saros. *Good bye to Elsa*. Delhi, 1975.

Dalal, Nergis. *The Inner Door*. Delhi, 1975.

Desai, Anita. *Voices in the City*. Delhi, 1965.

———. *Bye-bye Blackbird*. Delhi, 1971.

———. *Where Shall We Go This Summer?* Delhi, 1975.

———. *Fire on the Mountain*. U.S.A., 1977.

Desani, Govind V. *All About H. Hatterr*. London, 1948.

Futehally, Zeenuth. *Zohra*. Bombay, 1951.

Ghosh, Sudhin N. *And Gazelles Leaping*. London, 1948.

———. *The Flame of the Forest*. London, 1955.

Hosain, Attia. *Sunlight on a Broken Column*. London, 1961.

Jhabvala, Ruth Prawer. *To Whom She Will*. London, 1955.

———. *The Nature of Passion*. London, 1956.

———. *Esmond in India*. London, 1958.

———. *Get Ready for Battle*. Suffolk, 1983. First publ. 1962.

———. *A Backward Place*. Delhi, 1965.

———. *A New Dominion*. London, 1972.

———. *Heat and Dust*. Delhi, 1975.

———. *In Search of Love and Beauty*. London, 1983.

———. *The Householder*. Delhi, 1960.

———. *A Stronger Climate*. London, 1968.

———. *Like Birds, Like Fishes*. London, 1963.

———. *An Experience of India*. London, 1971.

———. *How I Became a Holy Mother and Other Stories*. Suffolk, 1976.
———. *Three Continents*. London, 1987.
Joshi, Arun. *The Strange Case of Billy Biswas*. Delhi, 1971.
———. *The Foreigner*. Delhi, 1968.
———. *The Apprentice*. Delhi, 1974.
Malgonkar, Manohar. *Combat of Shadows*. London, 1962.
———. *Distant Drum*. New Delhi, 1960.
———. *A Bend in the Ganges*. New Delhi, 1964.
———. *The Princes*. London, 1970.
———. *A Toast in Warm Wine*. Delhi, 1974.
———. *Bombay Beware*. Delhi, 1975.
———. *Open Season*. Delhi, 1978.
———. *Bandicoot Run*. Delhi, 1982.
Markandaya, Kamala. *Nectar in a Sieve*. Bombay, 1955.
———. *Some Inner Fury*. London, 1957.
———. *A Silence of Desire*. London, 1961.
———. *Possession*. London, 1963.
———. *A Handful of Rice*. Delhi, 1966.
———. *The Coffer Dams*. Delhi, 1969.
———. *The Nowhere Man*. London, 1973.
———. *The Two Virgins*. Vikas, Delhi, 1977. First publ. 1974.
———. *The Golden Honeycomb*. New York, 1978.
Mehta, Ved. *Walking the Indian Streets*. London, 1960.
Naipaul, V.S. *An Area of Darkness*. London, 1964.
———. *India: A Wounded Civilization*. Great Britain, 1977.
Narayan, R.K. *The Guide*. First publ. 1958.
———. *The Man-Eater of Malgudi*. U.S.A. 1961.
———. *The Painter of Signs*. U.S.A. 1976.
———. *My Dateless Diary*. Delhi, 1969. First publ. 1960.
———. *Next Sunday*. Delhi, 1960.
———. *Reluctant Guru*. Delhi, 1974.
———. *Lawley Road*. Delhi.
———. *A Horse and Two Goats*. Delhi, 1970.
———. *Waiting for the Mahatma*. Delhi. First publ. 1955.
Rajan, Balachandra. *The Dark Dancer*. London, 1959.
———. *Too Long in the West*. Bombay, 1961.
Rao, Raja. *Kanthapura*. Delhi, 1977. First publ. 1938
———. *The Serpent and the Rope*. New Delhi, 1960.
———. *The Cat and Shakespeare*. Delhi, 1971. First publ. 1965.
———. *The Policeman and the Rose*. Delhi, 1978.
Rau, Santha Rama. *Remember the House*. London, 1956.
Sahgal, Nayantara. *The Day in Shadow*. New Delhi, 1973.
———. *Prison and Chocolate Cake*. 1954.
———. *A Storm in Chandigarh*. London, 1969.

———. *A Time to be Happy*. Delhi. First publ. 1958.
———. *This Time of Morning*. London, 1965.
———. *A Situation in New Delhi*. London, 1977.
Singh, Khushwant. *Train to Pakistan*. London, 1956.
———. *I Shall Not Hear the Nightingale*. London, 1959.
———. *A Bride for the Sahib*. New Delhi, 1967.

B. SECONDARY SOURCES

Books

Abrams, M.H. *A Glossary of Literary Terms*. New York, 1971.
Agarwal, R.C. *Constitutional History of India and National Movement*. New Delhi, 1981.
Amirthanayagam, Guy, ed. *Writers in East-West Encounter: New Cultural Bearings*. Hong Kong, 1982.
Amur, G.S. *Manohar Malgonkar*. New Delhi, 1973.
Anand, Mulk Raj. *The King-Emperor's English or The Role of the English Language in Free India*. Bombay, 1948.
Baig, Tara Ali. *India's Woman Power*. Delhi, 1973.
Bearce, George D. *British Attitudes Towards India* (1784-1858). Oxford, 1961.
Buck, Pearl S. *My Several Worlds*. Methuen, New York, 1955.
Chandrashekhar, K.R. *Bhabani Bhattacharya*. New Delhi, 1974.
Cowasjee, Saros. *So Many Freedoms*. Delhi, 1977.
Derrett, M.E. *The Modern Indian Novel in English: A Comparative Approach*. Brussels, 1966.
Gokak, V.K. *English in India, Its Present and Future*. Bombay, 1964.
Greenberger, Allen J. *The British Image of India*. London, 1969.
Harrex, S.C. *The Fire and the Offering: The English Language Novel of India*. Vols. I & II. Calcutta, 1978.
Hemenway, Stephen. *The Novel of India*, Vols. I & II. Calcutta, 1975.
Iyenger, K.R. Srinivas. *Indian Writing in English*. Delhi, 1984. First publ. 1962.
Joseph, Margaret P. *Kamala Markandaya*. New Delhi, 1980.
Kulkarni, V.B. *British Statesmen in India*. Delhi, 1961.
Lal, P. *The Alien Insiders: Indian Writing in English*. Calcutta, 1979.
Lodge, David. *The Language of Fiction*. London, 1966.
McCutchion, David. *Indian Writing in English*. Calcutta, 1969.
Mehta, P.P. *Indo-Anglian Fiction: An Assessment*. Bareilly, 1968.
Melwani, Murli Das. *Themes in Indo Anglian Literature*. Bareilly, 1977.
———. *Critical Essays*. Calcutta, 1971.
Menon, V.P. *The Story of the Integration of the Indian States*. Delhi, 1961.
Mitchell, Basil, ed. *The Philosophy of Religion*. Oxford, 1971.
Mohan, Ramesh. *Indian Writing in English*. Madras, 1978.
Mukherjee, Meenakshi. *The Twice-Born Fiction*. New Delhi, 1974.

Naik, M.K., ed. *Aspects of Indian Writing in English*. Madras, 1979.

Naik, M.K. *et al. Critical Essays on Indian Writing in English*. Madras, 1977.

Narasimhaiah, C.D. ed. *The Swan and the Eagle*. Simla, 1969.

Nicholson, Kai. *A Presentation of Social Problems in the Indo-Anglian and Anglo-Indian Novel*. Bombay, 1972.

Parameswaram, Uma. *A Study of Representative Indo-English Novelists*. New Delhi, 1976.

Parsons, L. and E. Shils. *Towards a General Theory of Action*. Massachusetts, 1951.

Press, John, ed. *Commonwealth Literature*. Heinemann, 1965.

Punckar, S. Mokashi. *The Indo-Anglian Creed*. Calcutta, 1972.

Pyles, Thomas. *The Origin and Development of the English Language*. New York, 1971.

Radhakrishnan, S. *East and West: Some Reflections*. London, 1954.

Ramakrishna, D. ed. *Indian English Prose*. Delhi, 1980.

Rao, A.V. Krishna. *The Indo-Anglian Novel and the Changing Tradition*. Mysore, 1972.

Roy Choudhary, S.C. *Social, Cultural and Economic History of India*. New Delhi, 1980.

———. *History of Modern India*. New Delhi, 1980.

Shahane, V.A. *Ruth Prawer Jhabvala*. New Delhi, 1976.

Sharma, G.P. *Nationalism in Indo-Anglian Fiction*. New Delhi, 1978.

Sharma, K.K. *Indo-English Literature: A Collection of Critical Essays on Indian Creative Writers in English*. Ghaziabad, 1977.

Singar, Milton, ed. *Introducing Indian Liberal Education*. Chicago, 1957.

Singh, Bhupal. *A Survey of Anglo-Indian Fiction*. London, 1939.

Sinha, K.N., ed. *Indian Writing in English*. New Delhi, 1976.

Singh, R.S. *Indian Novel in English*. New Delhi, 1977.

Spencer, Dorothy. *Indian Fiction in English*. Philadelphia, 1960.

Spear, Percival. *A History of India*. 2 Vols. Great Britain, 1970.

Spear, T.G. Percival. *The Nabobs: A Study of the Social Life of the English in 18th Century India*. Great Britain, 1932.

Steel, Flora Annie. *The Hosts of the Lord*. N.D.

Thapar, Romila. *Ancient Indian Social History: Some Interpretations*. Delhi, 1978.

Thompson, Edward. *An End of the Hours*. N.D.

Trevelyan, G.M. *History of England*. O.M. Longman, N.D.

Ullman, Stephen. *Language and Style*. Oxford, 1966.

Verghese, C. Paul. *Nirad C. Chaudhari*. New Delhi, 1973.

———. *Problems of the Indian Creative Writer in English*. Bombay, 1971.

Vivekananda, Swami. *The Teachings of Swami Vivekananda*, 4 Vols. Calcutta, 1971.

Walsh, William. *Readings in Commonwealth Literature*. Oxford, 1973.

Williams, Haydn Moore. *Studies in Modern Indian Fiction in English*. 2 Vols.

Calcutta, 1973.
———. *Indo-Anglian Literature (1800-1970) A Survey*. Madras, 1976.
———. *The Fiction of Ruth Prawer Jhabvala*. Calcutta, 1973.

Journals

Adkins, Joan F. "History as Art Form: Khushwant Singh's *Train to Pakistan*." *Journal of Indian Writing in English*, Vol. 2, No. 2, July 1974.

Agarwal, Ramlal. "Forster, Jhabvala and Readers." *Journal of Indian Writing in English*, Vol. 3, No. 2, July, 1975.

Anand, Mulk Raj. "Old Myths and New Myths: Recital Versus Novel." *The Literary Criterion*, XII, 1976, Nos. 2-3.

Appasamy, S.P. "*The Golden Honeycomb*· A Saga of Princely India by Kamala Markandaya." *Journal of Indian Writing in English*, Vol. 6, No. 2, July 1978.

Argyle, Barry. "Kamala Markandaya's *Nectar in a Sieve*." *Ariel*, Vol. 4, No. 1.

Asnani, Shyam M. "Jhabvala's Novels." *Journal of Indian Writing in English*, Vol. 2, No. 1, Jan. 1974.

Belliappa, Meena. "A Study of Jhabvala's Fiction." *The Banasthali Patrika*, No. 12, Year 4, Jan. 1969.

Berry, Margaret. "India: A Double Key." *Journal of Indian Writing in English*, Vol. 6, No. 1, Jan. 1978.

Bhattacharya, Bhabani. "Women in my Stories." *Journal of Indian Writing in English*, Vol. 3, No. 2, July 1975.

Blackwell, Fritz. "Perception of the Guru in the Fiction of Jhabvala." *Journal of Indian Writing in English*, Vol. 5, No. 2, July 1977.

Chaddah, R.P. "The Partition in Indo-Anglian Fiction." *Journal of Indian Writing in English*, Vol. 5, No. 2, July 1977.

Chauhan, P.S. "Kamala Markandaya." *The Literary Criterion*, XII, Nos. 2-3, 1976.

Du Bois, Cora. "The Cultural Interplay between East and West." *The East and West Must Meet: A Symposium* (East Lansing, Michigan, 1959).

Fisher, Marlene. "Mulk Raj Anand's Confessional Novels." *Journal of Indian Writing in English*, Vol. 4, No. 2, July 1976.

Goonaratne, Yasmin. "Satirical Semi-Colour: Ruth Prawer Jhabvala's Screenplay for *Bombay Talkie*." *Journal of Indian Writing in English*, Vol. 8, Nos. 1-2, Jan.-July 1980).

Gupta, Balarama G.S. "Some Reflections on Indian Writing in English." *Journal of Indian Writing in English*, Vol. 1, No. 2, July 1973.

Gupta, Rameshwar, *et al*. "Indo-English Literature: Some Views." *The Banasthali Patrika*, No. 12, Year 4, Jan. 1969.

Iyengar, K.R. Srinivas. "English and English Studies in India." *Journal of Indian Writing in English*, Vol. 2, No. 1, Jan. 1974.

Kamani, Chetan. "Nirad Chaudhuri's Style." *Journal of Indian Writing in*

English.

Kumar, Shiv K. "Tradition and Change in the Novels of Kamala Markandaya." *Books Abroad*.

Kushwaha, M.S. "A Neglected Area of Indo-Anglian Writing." *Journal of Indian Writing in English*, Vol. 6, No. 1, Jan. 1978.

Lal, P. "Nostalgia Indo-Anglia." *Journal of Indian Writing in English*, Vol. 3, No. 1, Jan. 1975.

Madhavan. A. "For Whom Do We Write." *The Literary Criterion*, XII, Nos. 2-3, 1976.

Montgomery, Ruth. "Kamala Markandaya's *Nectar in a Sieve*." *Wilson Library Bulletin*, XXVIII, Nov. 1963.

Mukherjee, Sujit. Indian-English Literature in the Classroom." *The Literary Criterion*, XII, Nos. 2-3, 1976.

Pollard, Arthur. "Kamala Markandaya's *The Golden Honeycomb*." *Journal of Indian Writing in English*, Vol. 8, Nos. 1-2, Jan-July 1980.

Rao, K.S.N. "Some Notes on the Plots of Kamala Markandaya's Novels." *Indian Literature*, XII, No. 1, 1970.

———. "Markandaya's *Possession* and the Idea of the Triumph of the Spirit." *The Indian P.E.N.*, XXXV, Nov. 1969.

Rau, Santha Rama. "New Voices from Asia." *American Association of University Women Journal* (New York), Oct. 1964.

Ramamurti, K.S. "Bankim Chandra and the Indian Novel in English." *Journal of Indian Writing in English*, 6, No. 2, July 1978.

Sircar, Arjya. "The Crisis in Indo-Anglian Fiction: The Linguistic Aspect." *Commonwealth Quarterly*, Dec. 1978.

Shahane, Vasant A. "Jhabvala and the Indian Scene." *Journal of Indian Writing in English*, Vol. 4, No. 2, July 1976.

———. "Indo-Anglian Fiction and the Question of Form." *Journal of Indian Writing in English*, 2, No. 2, July 1974.

———. "Heat and Dust." *The Banasthali Patrika*, No. 21, Year 9, July 1976.

———. "An Artist's Experience of India: Ruth Prawer Jhabvala's Fiction." *The Literary Criterion*, XII, Nos. 2-3, 1976.

Shimer, Dorothy B. "Bhabani Bhattacharya: Gandhi Biographer." *Journal of Indian Writing in English*, Vol. 2, No. 2, July 1974.

Thumboo, Edwin. "Kamala Markandaya's *A Silence of Desire*." *Journal of Indian Writing in English*, Nos. 1-2, Vol. 8, Jan.-July 1980.

Varady Evelyn. "American and British Response to Anita Desai's *Games at Twilight and Other Stories*." *Journal of Indian Writing in English*, 8, Nos. 1-2, Jan.-July 1980.

Verghese, Paul C. "A Note on *Esmond in India*." *Journal of Indian Writing in English*, 4, No. 2, July 1976.

———. "Problems of the Indian Novelist in English." *The Banasthali Patrika*, No. 12, Year 4, Jan. 1969.

White, Robin. "Fiction in India." *The Reporter*. 28, No. 4, 1963.